From
A Barren
Mango Orchard

A Story of God's Faithfulness

A Roman Catholic Architect from Austria,
A Southern Baptist Lady from Georgia,
A Pentecostal Preacher from India,
and a Mango Orchard
that won't grow. . .

What can God do with these?

Read the Amazing Story.

by
George Chavanikamannil

(aka: "Uncle" George)

Dedicated to:

**My beloved Leelamma,
who has been my faithful better half
for over 50 years.**

Preface

This book is the result of my feeble attempt to narrate the story of God's faithfulness. Many who know us and our story have encouraged us to write it down. I must confess that I am not gifted with the talent or ability to write. Therefore, I kept postponing it while promising friends who asked for it that I would get it done "one of these days!"

As I approached the 75th year of my life, God put a desire in my heart to finally write the story down. I have tried my best to make it as simple as possible. I hope I have succeeded in that. You are the judge!

There are so many that I need to thank for making this story possible.

First, all the glory, honor, and thanks belong to my Lord Jesus Christ, who came seeking me and gave His life for me so that I might become His child, live for Him, and serve Him. I do not have words to thank Him for all the blessings with which He has blessed me ever since I met Him in person back in 1967, when I was nineteen years old. I cannot even imagine a life without my Lord Jesus Christ. Finding Him, or rather, being found by Him, is undoubtedly the greatest blessing of my life. My passion is to be faithful to Him and hear the words "well done, good and faithful servant" when I stand before Him in glory!

The second highest blessing in my life is my beloved, my best friend, and partner in life for the past fifty years, Leelamma. I have known Leela, as she prefers to be called, for almost all my life. We were born and raised in the same small village in the Southern tip of India. My first memory of her is when she was about four or five years old! God blessed me to have her as my life partner, though I do not at all deserve her by any means. Without a shadow of a doubt, all that I am and have accomplished in life and ministry is due to

4

her. I cannot thank her enough for the incredible person she has been all these years and for being the best help-mate that any man can wish for. I love you far more than you will ever know, and I praise God daily for blessing me with you.

Then there are the two most wonderful sons, Finny and Renny, and their two blessed spouses, Laura and Roshini, and the nine VERY precious grandchildren- Luke, Ethan, Timothy, Tabitha, John, Peter, Daniel, Bethany, and Matthew. How blessed we are because of them! The greatest joy Leela and I have is that they all love and serve the Lord Jesus. God has blessed our sons and their families far more than we ever expected or even prayed for! As you will read later in our story, one of the fears the enemy put in our hearts to discourage us from obeying the Lord's call to North India was the fear of our children's future. Specifically, the fear was concerning their education. From childhood, both are brilliant. How we could send them to good universities if we went to India was a question that plagued us. Time and space do not permit us to tell the miraculous stories of God's provisions to provide an excellent education for our children.

If God has called you, step out in faith, and you will see the glory of God. Only if we step out from our safety zone can we see the Lord working to reveal His glory.

The Holy Scripture is full of illustrations of this principle. Only when the children of Israel stepped into the waters of the Jordan did the river part. Only after the stone was removed from the tomb of Lazarus did Jesus raise him up. When we obey Him, He takes over and does the rest. We, too, are witnesses to this principle. If we had held on to our jobs and not obeyed the Lord, our children would not have received all the blessings they enjoy now. All glory to God!

I must say special thanks to our parents and siblings for their role in making us who we are. Leela's parents, who were pastors, have always been great prayer warriors on our behalf. Her father is resting with the Lord now. While alive, he greatly encouraged us to pursue the Lord's call on our lives. Leela's mother, who is 93, faithfully prays for us daily. We owe a huge debt of gratitude to both of them.

My parents had dedicated me in my childhood to the Lord's work. They desired to see me as a clergyman in the Church of South India (CSI). They sacrificed immensely to educate me. They both are now resting with the Lord. I still miss them very much and wish they could have seen all the amazing blessings with which the Lord has blessed us, our children, and the ministries in India.

Both my siblings loved me deeply. They both are resting in the Lord now. My sister, fourteen years older than me, cared for me in my childhood. I was so attached to her that I insisted on going with her when she went on her honeymoon! My brother, twelve years older than me, was passionate about seeing me educated well. He instilled in me a desire to learn English as a child. He was a schoolteacher. Whenever he came home for holidays, he would bring a handful of books (when books were costly and hard to get) and taught me how to read and write English. I owe a huge debt of gratitude to my brother (and to Kochamma, his wife) for their love and investments in my life.

Scores of brothers and sisters in the Lord ought to be thanked by name, as so many have helped us in different ways. That would make this way too long. So, I ask your pardon. The Lord has recorded in His book what you have done for us, and He will reward you for sure.

I must mention three congregations in the US by name, as these churches played very special roles in our lives.

First, the Jackson Street Assembly of God Church in St. Paul, Minnesota. That congregation was our "family" when none of our relatives could be with us and help us when we moved to the US. Leela and I got married there on September 1, 1973. The Pastors and members of that small congregation rallied around us and did everything for us. We will never forget their kindness to us. We especially thank Anne Michaelson (now Anne Alexander) and Beverly Clemens for their sacrificial help.

Second, Pasadena Foursquare Church. When we moved to California in 1974 and were struggling financially, Pastor Maurice Tolle and the church came to our help. The parsonage of the church became our home for the next five years. Both our children were born when we lived at 182 Harkness Avenue, Pasadena. We can never forget that church family that stood with us during some of the most challenging days of our lives in the US.

Third, West Los Angeles Christian Center. Pastor Herb and Judy Maydwell warmly welcomed us and made us part of that loving family. We first met them in 1975 through what I believe is a sovereign miracle (the story is told in Chapter 7, *A Miracle Through the Los Angeles Yellow Pages*). They opened the doors of many congregations of Christian Evangelistic Assemblies (CEA), now known as Grace International Churches and Ministries, to us. That eventually led us to become part of CEA. I received my ordination to the Christian ministry through CEA in 1984.

Both Karl Mantl and Craig Reynolds, who played vital roles in finding the land in Dehradun, were members of this congregation. (Details are narrated in Chapters 14 and 15).

Pastor Herb and Judy are now resting in the Lord. We will forever be grateful to them for their love and friendship. After all these years, our sons still remember West LA Christian Center as the best church they have been part of, especially the potluck dinners there!

We must wholeheartedly thank all of our colleagues in India. As seen in the following pages, many worked hard and sacrificed much to fulfill our vision. Without their hard work, we could not have accomplished anything at all. We are not naming any here. We want to say a BIG "thank you" to all of them and pray for the Lord's very best for them.

Thanks to Mrs. Linda Enwald for her help in editing what I wrote. I am grateful to her for her kind help. While I remain responsible for all the imperfections in this work, Mrs. Enwald made it much better than it was. May the Lord bless her!

Our dear friends Craig Reynolds and Bindu Gijy worked many hours to format my helter-skelter writing. Sincere thanks to both of you. May the Lord bless you both!

Special thanks also to our very good friend, Dr. Timothy Tennent, President of Asbury Theological Seminary, who has played a vital role in our story for reading the manuscript and encouraging us to publish it.

We pray that the following pages will bless you and encourage you to love the Lord with all your heart, mind, soul, and strength and serve Him faithfully.

As Apostle Paul wrote in 1 Corinthians 15:58: *"Therefore, my beloved brothers, be steadfast, immovable, always abounding in the work of the Lord, knowing that in the Lord your labor is not in vain.*

January 25, 2024
"Uncle" George".

Soli Deo Gloria!

The greatest blessings that the Lord has granted us are our two godly sons, their godly spouses, and our nine grandchildren. We continually praise the Lord for them and give all glory to God alone!

Chapter 1

Childhood

Our story begins in the South Indian state of Kerala, known as "God's own country." [1]

My wife, Leela, and I were born and raised in traditional Saint Thomas Christian families. We are also known as Syrian Christians. We believe that Saint Thomas, also known as "doubting Thomas," one of the twelve Apostles of Christ, came to India in 52 AD, preached the Gospel of our Lord Jesus Christ, and established several churches in the South West tip of India before he died the death of a martyr. It is our ardent faith that he baptized our forefathers.

Born and raised in the Syrian Orthodox Church (Jacobite), my great-grandfather heard the Gospel preached by CMS missionaries and was born again and joined the Anglican church (then known as CMS). It later became CSI-Church of South India [2].

---

[1] Kerala, which means "land of coconuts," is the name adopted for the state on November 1, 1956, under the *States Reorganization Act,* when Malabar was merged with Travancore Cochin to form the new state. The state's original name was from the two kingdoms that joined the Union of India after independence in 1947- Travancore and Cochin. "God's Own Country" is the slogan that the government of Kerala uses to promote tourism. Kerala ("Keralam" in Malayalam) is an amazingly beautiful place. Billy Graham, a person who has traveled the world more than most of us, describes Kerala as the most beautiful place that he has seen in his autobiography, *Just As I Am*! No small commendation coming from such a person as Billy Graham! For the sake of ease of communication, we will use the word Kerala all through the narrative.

[2] Church Missionary Society (CMS) was founded on April 12, 1799, by William Wilberforce, Henry Thornton, and Thomas Babington. The

Leela's parents belonged to the Mar Thoma (Saint Thomas) Church. The Mar Thoma Church resulted from a reformation in the Syrian Orthodox/Jacobite Church in 1887.[3]

We are also known as Syrian Christians because of our community's connection with Syria's ancient Christian community for centuries. Through this bond, the liturgy of the Syrian Orthodox/Jacobite Church was in Syriac for centuries.[4]

Our parents were godly and raised both of us in fear of the Lord. Leela's parents were among the first in our village to receive believers' baptism due to the influence of the revival that broke out in Kerala through the preaching of the Brotheren and Pentecostal preachers. Leela's father, Mr. K. I. George, was ordained as a pastor in the Indian Pentecostal Church and faithfully pastored several churches

---

society's Original name was "Society for Missions in Africa and the East." The name CMS was adopted in 1812.

[3] The reformation within the Orthodox/Jacobite Church is an amazing story of the power of the Word of God. The Church existed with just the liturgy for centuries, and that too in Syriac, a language that most people did not understand. Only tiny portions of the Holy Bible were translated into the language of the common people until the Western Protestant Missionaries came to Kerala. When the Bible was translated into Malayalam and priests in the mother Church read it, a few of them began to question customs and practices within the Church that were contrary to the Holy Bible. A group of them, under the leadership of Palakunnathu Abraham Malpan (1796-1845), who is now known as the Martin Luther of the East, began to preach and teach that these customs and practices are contrary to the teachings of the Holy Bible and therefore, must be rejected. Many people joined with the priests and began to read the Holy Bible in their heart language. Eventually, the movement became what is known today as the Mar Thoma Church.

[4] Syriac is the language of ancient Syria. It is a western dialect of Aramaic, the mother tongue of Jesus.

until he was called home by the Lord in 1994. He was a sincere and faithful man of God who faced much opposition, primarily from his siblings and father-in-law, for leaving the Mar Thoma Church and embracing the Pentecostal doctrine. He stood firm in his convictions and raised all his children in the fear of the Lord, Leela being the oldest of seven.

Our Parents

My parents were active members of the local CMS church.[5] My father served as a lay minister in that church occasionally. My maternal grandmother was a member of the Jacobite Church. As children, we spent a lot of time with her, and thus, we were privileged to grow up imbibing both the Eastern and Western Christian traditions. One of my maternal uncles was my grandmother's parish priest. As a small boy, I

---

[5] Church of South India (CSI) was formed on September 27, 1947, as an ecumenical church from the union of the Anglican Church (CMS), Methodist Church, South India United Church, and Basel Mission Churches in South India.

loved to attend worship services in my grandmother's church. The colorful priestly garments, beautiful sounds of the Syriac liturgy[6], the sweet smell of incense, and the rituals all live vividly in my memory even after all these decades!

Good Friday service lasted almost the whole day and culminated with the congregation eating together. The meal was a simple rice gruel served on banana leaves. We would dig a hole in the ground and keep the banana leaf on top to keep the gruel from spilling. The banana leaf becomes a deep bowl when the hot gruel is served! All of us, rich or poor, would sit together in rows on the grass in front of the church and participate in that special meal. What sweet memories of childhood!

I am the youngest of three in my family; the oldest was our only sister, Leelamma (official name C.G. Achamma), and then my only brother, Joy (official name C.G. Oommen)[7]. I am fourteen years younger than my sister

---

[6] The survival of the Syrian Orthodox/Jacobite Church amid the predominantly Hindu population of South India is indeed a miracle story. If tradition is to be believed, St. Thomas came to present-day Kerala in 52 AD. There were waves of immigration from Syria and other parts of the "Middle East" to India in the early Christian centuries. The Christian community flourished through the centuries even though the Holy Bible was not translated into the people's language. The Church survived just with the liturgy! And that liturgy was in Syriac, a language ordinary people did not understand!

[7] The custom of naming children in Syrian Christian families is very fascinating. The oldest son is given the paternal grandfather's name, and the oldest daughter is given the paternal grandmother's name. Oommen was the name of our paternal grandfather, and Achamma was the name of our paternal grandmother. The second name of all children will be that of the father. In most cases, that would be kept as an initial along with family name or surname, as in the case of my brother and sister- the letter "C" standing for our family name, Chavanikamannil, and "G" standing for George, our father's first name. The second son would be

and twelve years younger than my brother. My parents lost two daughters in infancy, one older than me and one younger. My older sister passed away before I was born. Her name was Mary, named after our maternal grandmother, according to our custom. I have vague memories of my younger sister's passing. Her name was Mini. My brother named her Mini after reading the famous short story, *Kabuli Wala*, by the Nobel Prize-winning Indian author Rabindranath Tagore (1861-1941). To this day, that name, Mini, is very special to me. My little sister died because medical care was very inadequate in our small village. We had to walk around two miles to the nearest small clinic. By the time medical care was given to her, she was too ill to survive.

I look forward to meeting in glory both of my sisters, who passed away before they had a chance to grow up. What a glorious day that will be when we will see all our dear ones who have gone on to glory before us! Above all, on that day, we will see the One who died for us on the Cross of Calvary! And He will wipe away every tear from our eyes.[8]

My childhood was very joyous even though we had few material things compared to many children today. My father was an art teacher in a local private school. We also had some land with various trees and plants, such as coconut

---

named after the maternal grandfather, and the second daughter after the maternal grandmother. If there were more children, they would be named after uncles and aunts. In my case, I was named Kuruvilla after my maternal grandfather. However, the Principal of the first school where I studied changed my name when he wrote the transfer certificate (TC). Instead of writing my name as Kuruvilla C. George in the TC, he wrote George Kuruvila C, effectively altering my name forever. When I applied for a passport, my family name needed to be written out in complete form; thus, I became George Kuruvila Chavanikamannil!

[8] Revelation 21:4.

trees, black pepper, mangos, cashew nuts, tapioca, and various vegetables.

In my childhood, I had severe eczema. It was a common ailment for many children in our village. In my case, the problem was severe. Because of the severity of eczema, no one liked to carry or touch me except for my parents and two older siblings. I am told that the only other person who would touch or hold me was my father's younger brother, our next-door neighbor.

By God's grace, growing up, we never knew hunger, while many in our village did. Our little farm produced most of the things we needed. Black pepper, cashew nuts, coconuts, and seasonal vegetables that grew on the family farm provided enough cash to purchase the rice and other essential groceries. So, though we were not rich, I grew up thinking we were because, compared to many of my childhood friends, our lives were very comfortable. My parents were generous people who helped our neighbors who struggled for their meals. I grew up seeing our mother and father giving things away to needy people.

When I was a small boy, barter system was still prevalent in my village. That leads me to a memorable story from my childhood.

From the time I can remember, I was fond of peanuts. (I must confess that I still like them as an older adult; all my close friends know that peanut butter is still one of my favorites!) Even though we grew plenty of cashews, our part of Kerala did not grow peanuts (or, as we call it in India, groundnuts! They come from the ground, right?)

We had small shops in the village that would barter cashew for peanuts- two peanuts for one cashew! We thought that it was a great deal for us. We children had no idea that the merchants were taking advantage of us; peanuts were much cheaper than cashews. But we didn't know that. Moreover, we had plenty of cashew nuts. We just needed to pick them up from the ground around the cashew trees without being caught by our parents!

Once the cashew season is over, no more cashews are readily available. We had to wait a whole year until the next season to eat peanuts as we had no money to buy them!

My father had a habit. He wouldn't sell cashews in the season as the price was low then. So, he would store them in giant clay jars in one of the rooms of our house. And he would sell when the price went up after the cashew season.

One day, I began to crave peanuts. I knew there were plenty of cashews stored inside my house. If only I could get hold of a few without my parents knowing!

So, I waited for my parents to become busy with their daily chores and, at an opportune time, sneaked into the room where they had stored all the cashews. I gently opened the back window and began to drop cashews into the backyard. I became greedy and took a whole bunch of cashews. Then I got out as if nothing had happened and slowly went to the backyard to complete my stealth operation, eager to collect all the cashews and run to the nearest peanut shop.

But, when I reached the backyard, guess who was standing there with a nice cane in her hand? My mother! I will never forget that day. I can tell you for sure that I learned my lesson that day. I have never stolen anything from anyone since that memorable day.

I thank God for my parents, who taught me right and wrong from childhood. They never abused me. But they did punish me when I did wrong. I believe we ignore the Scriptural principle taught in Proverbs 13:24 and related passages to our peril.[9] Loving discipline is essential in bringing up a godly generation.

Our village had no electricity or paved roads. I studied by kerosene lamps until I went off to the University. The mode of transportation was either walk or bullock carts! All the supplies, such as groceries, were brought to the village by bullock carts or people carrying them in big baskets or sacks on their heads. Our next-door neighbor had a bullock cart and a small grocery shop. It was unforgettable fun whenever we got to ride in his cart! He would travel about 25 kilometers to the nearest wholesale market weekly to procure goods. It took a whole day and a night for the roundtrip!

Indoor plumbing was unheard of in our community. I remember well my mother's reaction when she first saw a toilet inside a house. She couldn't believe it as she thought of the bathroom as filthy and to be kept far away from the house!

All cooking was by fire. "Stove" was three stones set up to support pots and pans with fire beneath them. The kitchen was a place of smoke and soot. Coconut trees supplied primary fuel- branches, leaves, the husk surrounding and protecting the nut, and the nut's hard shell are all used as fuel for the fire! Because every part of the coconut tree is valuable, fascinating myths developed in Indian mythology about the creation of coconut trees.[10]

---

[9] Proverbs 13:24; 19:18; 22:15; 23:13,14; 29:15.

[10] Most famous of these is the story of Trishanku, a saintly man who desired to go to heaven bodily, Vishwamitra, the sage who helped him, and Indra, the god who refused him admission into heaven. The Gist of the myth is that Trishanku, suspended between heaven and earth as Indra refused him admission to heaven, was transformed into a coconut tree by Vishwamitra!

Every fairly well-to-do family had its own well. We had two wells in our property- one very close to the house and another about a hundred yards away. During monsoon rains, there would be so much water in the wells that they would overflow. But during very severe summers, both our wells would run dry. Then we had to walk as much as a mile to fetch water! One of my chores as a boy was helping my mother draw water out of the well and carrying it to the kitchen. I was also partly responsible for procuring fodder for our goats and cows. I loved to climb trees to cut leaves for the goats. As I was lean and tall, climbing trees was easy for me. My ability and joy in climbing trees became helpful in the ministry of the Gospel later in my life.

One of the stories I often heard growing up was about my stealing away to school at two or three. (Of the incident I have a very vague memory, probably implanted from hearing the story told by my mother). My sister was 14 years older than me, and my brother twelve years. They both went to school as well as my father as he was a teacher. At the age of two, I insisted that I must also go to school. As I was too young, the school would not admit me. So, one day I sneaked out of the house without my mother noticing and went to school! The school was less than half a mile away, and everyone in the school knew our family as my father was a teacher there. So, one of the teachers welcomed me and allowed me to sit in the class with the other children.

My mother panicked when she couldn't find me at home. She immediately guessed that I must have sneaked away to school as I was always demanding to go to school when my siblings and father went to school. When she arrived, sure enough, I was sitting in a class barely dressed! (In those days, in our village, children as young as I, wore hardly any clothes at all!)

Because of my eagerness to go to school and study, my parents decided to invite a "guru"[11] to come and teach me at home when I was three or four. When the guru started to come to teach me, other parents in our neighborhood who had children of the same age asked my parents whether they also could be allowed to join. So, our guru taught about seven or eight children in our neighborhood, in our little "school."[12]

We sat on the floor and wrote with our fingers in the sand spread in front of us! All the children together would recite each letter and number aloud. Our guru would use a very sharp iron instrument and write each letter and number we learned on a particular kind of dry palm leaf. That was our "book." One leaf would contain only a few alphabets or numbers. When the first leaf was full, another leaf would be added. My "book" soon became very thick as more and more leaves were added because I was a quick learner, I am told.

I had my "book" for many years, as this palm leaf is very durable. In the olden days, before pen and paper became readily available, that was the way of keeping all records, including legal documents.

Everyone greatly respected gurus. When a man or a woman got married, their guru would be a chief guest. The bride/groom would give him a gift just before s/he stepped out of the house to go to get married. Guru, in turn, would

---

[11] The word "Guru" means teacher. Guru is a Sanskrit word. In our mother tongue, Malayalam, the word is "Aasan." It was customary in those days for parents who could afford to employ a "guru" to privately teach their children the alphabet and numbers before enrolling in a formal school. I still have very vivid and loving memories of my "guru." He was a very kind person, though very strict.

[12] Such schools are known as "Ezhuthu Kalari"- which literally means, "writing place" or "place where one learns to write."

bless his student.[13] That custom is still prevalent. Years later, at the age of twenty-five, I also invited my guru to come and bless me and gave him a gift just before I set out on my journey to the US to get married.

Another incident that vividly lives in my memory happened when I was about five. I was a very naughty boy. My mother often used to tell me that I did not know how to walk; instead, I always ran. As a child, I was also very clumsy. Falling and getting hurt was almost like a hobby for me. Even now, I have scars on my knees to prove that!

Every one of the families around us, including ours, grew a lot of cassava, or as we used to call it, "kappa" or tapioca.[14] It was a staple food item for us, and preserving it after the harvest season till the next harvest was critical for our survival. The only way we could preserve it for a long time was by boiling it and then drying it very crisp. The harvest time of "kappa" was like a festival for us. It was very labor-intensive to uproot all the plants, separate the roots (it is the root of the cassava plant that is eaten, like a potato), peel them, cut them into small pieces, boil them, and spread them to dry. All neighboring families came together, and everyone worked all day and night, sometimes for several days and nights, depending on how large the harvest was. For us children, it was a very joyous time indeed.

My father's younger brother, Mr. M.O. Koshy, was our next-door neighbor. I used to call him "Uppappan"-

---

[13] This is known as "Gurudakshina" or "Guru Dakshina."

[14] Scientific name: Manihot esculenta Crantz. Known by names such as yuca, cassava, etc. is native to South America and belongs to the spurge family. It is called "kappa" or "maracheeni" in Malayalam and Simla Alu in Hindi. It was introduced to India by the Portuguese during the 17th century and to Kerala around 1880 by Thirunal Rama Varma, the Maharaja of Travancore, as a substitute for rice after a severe famine.

which means "father's younger brother."[15] One day the "kappa vattu"[16] was going on in his property. Every adult was busy working, and we children ran around. The process is usually near a well as a lot of water is needed for the work. As usual, I was running around. I had the habit of pretending to be a motor vehicle and would make engine noise and car horn noise etc., as I ran around. Around midnight or so, as I was pretending to drive my car, I fell into the well!

One of my cousins immediately jumped into the well and rescued me before I drowned. (I did not know how to swim). As he lifted me out of the deep water, I am reported to have said to him something like: "By the grace of God, nothing happened to me!" From then on, whenever he saw me, he would repeat that sentence and remind me how he rescued me.

Looking back, I can say for sure that it was the seal of the Holy Spirit on me that made me say those words, as I did not know Jesus as my Savior then. Had I perished that night in that well, I would have gone into an eternity without God. His hand of protection was on me, even though I did not recognize or acknowledge that until years later.

As children, we hardly had any toys. So, we became creative and made our toys. As we had plenty of coconut trees, coconut branches and leaves were our primary raw material for toys. We made balls out of the leaves and bullock carts and bulls out of the branches! We created and played our own games. When I see children, who have so many

---

[15] Our culture has distinct terms of respect for all relatives- the father's younger brother is "Uppappan," the older brother is "Perappan," the mother's brother is "Ammachan," etc. Hindi is even more elaborate. English is very poor in expressing relationships.

[16] The whole process was called "kappa vattu"- literally, boiling of kappa.

expensive toys and yet are bored of life, I praise God for my joyous childhood, even though I hardly had toys.

Life in our little village was peaceful and uneventful. About two miles away from our house, there was a Roman Catholic Church: St. John the Baptist Church. Every year the festival of St. John the Baptist was celebrated in that church for a week. It concluded with fireworks on Saturday night. That was the one major yearly event that we all looked forward to, Catholics, Protestants and even non-Christians.

The festival was the occasion for all from the surrounding villages and towns to purchase furniture, utensils, earthenware vessels, and any other household items they needed. We had no shopping malls, supermarkets, or even good shops anywhere near us. As there were no cars or buses, we all walked to the festival in colorful clothes. My father would give me one Rupee (about a quarter of a US dollar at that time) to spend as I wish! Oh! What great joy that was! I would buy a small rubber ball, a whistle, and some of my favorite snacks with that one Rupee. And I felt like a rich person! That rubber ball and whistle would last a few weeks before those are lost or broke. When that happened, there was immeasurable sorrow. From then on, I would look forward to the next year's festival and the one Rupee my father would give me!

Another great highlight of childhood was visiting my maternal grandmother. I never had the privilege of meeting my paternal grandmother. After giving birth to nine children- seven boys and two girls- she had passed away before I was born. My father was the third oldest among his siblings. My paternal grandfather, Mr. C. C. Oommen, was a very hard-working farmer who loved the Lord. I have many fond memories of him as he lived with us for a while, and my parents took care of him when he was elderly.

Our maternal grandmother lived in a place called Kanam, about ten miles away from our house. We would walk about two miles to the nearest bus stop and then take a bus. We had to walk another mile after we got down from the bus.

Our grandmother's house was near a large, beautiful rice field. I loved to be there with her. The scenic beauty of the land, so many different kinds of birds that sang melodiously, farmers plowing the rice field with their oxen, and the way they sang while working: all these put an indelible mark on my mind as a child. There were many different kinds of fruit trees on her property and also in the neighboring properties, which were all owned by our relatives. So many different types of mangoes! Getting up early in the morning to search for mangoes that fell from the trees at night was a joy. You had to get there before neighboring children got there! So, there was a spirit of competition also involved in it. Moreover, "Valliammachi,"[17] as I called her, always treated us to delicious meals!

Our grandmother's story is impressive indeed. She was married to my grandfather when she was just seven years old! And my grandfather was twelve! Even among Christians, child marriage was the norm of the day. She used to tell us many heart-warming stories of her life. Let me share with you one of my favorites.

Marriages were all "arranged" marriages in those days. The wedding usually took place in the groom's church. After a delicious marriage-feast for all the guests, the bride and groom and some guests would travel to the bride's home. The newly married couple would stay there for four days

---

[17] A common Malayalam word for Grandmother.

taking part in several special lunches and dinners given in their honor by various relatives.

On the fourth day, someone would come from the groom's home to take the newlyweds back to his place. Usually, it is an older relative that would come to accompany the bride and the groom. For some reason, it was a cousin of my grandfather, not much older than him, that came to take them back. As already said, there were no buses or cars in those days. All travel was by foot, and roads were not paved. The distance between the two homes was about ten miles.

The common custom was for men to walk ahead and women to follow behind. So, my grandfather and his cousin walked in front, and my grandmother (mind you, she is only seven!) walked behind them. The bride and the groom were both dressed in such a way that anyone who sees them would recognize that they were newly married.

As the men (boys, really) walked faster, gradually, the distance between the bride and the groom became farther and farther. After a little while, my grandmother noticed that an elephant was tied to a coconut tree not too far from her walking path. And she was deathly afraid of elephants! The moment she saw the elephant, she froze in fear, unable to take another step. She stood there and started crying. Of course, the groom and his cousin were far too ahead to notice all this. They kept walking, unaware that the bride was no longer walking behind them!

After a little while, an older gentleman came in the opposite direction. He saw the young boy dressed as a groom accompanied by one not much older than him merrily walking. He greeted them and passed them, assuming that the bride must be following, as the custom. After several minutes, he reached the little bride (my grandmother), frozen in fear of the elephant and crying. He understood what was happening. The man lifted my grandmother, put her on his shoulders, and ran after my grandfather and cousin! When he caught up with them, he scolded the groom and his cousin, told them to take care of the bride, and sent them on their way.

Whenever my grandmother told us that story, she had a special twinkle in her eyes. She became a widow at the age of 22! She already had two daughters and was carrying her third child when my grandfather passed away at 27 from pneumonia. My grandmother never remarried. She raised three daughters, overcoming many difficulties, and made sure that all three daughters were settled well.

My mother was the oldest daughter and was only three years old when my grandfather passed away.

Having only daughters in a "man's world" made life very difficult for my grandmother. My grandfather had quite a bit of land. Many people, including some close relatives, tried their best to cheat my grandmother out of the property. In His grace, God protected her and her three daughters from the schemes of the evil one because my grandmother solely depended on God. She was a woman of prayer. As a small child, I have witnessed her waking up regularly throughout the night and crying out to God.

My parents were blessed with the privilege of caring for our grandmother in her old age, just like they cared for our paternal grandfather in his old age. She lived with my parents for many years, once she became unable to live independently, and passed away in our home on July 12, 1982. She was in her 90s when she went to be with the Lord.

Let's never forget that there is a special blessing in honoring parents, especially when they are elderly and unable to care for themselves. The only commandment with a promise is the fifth commandment: *"Honor your father and your mother that your days may be long in the land that the LORD your God is giving you."* Exodus 20:12.

I sincerely believe that the Lord honored all of us children because our parents loved and obeyed the Lord and His Word. Not only did they sacrificially care for their elderly parents, but they also gave to the Lord and His servants generously even though they were not rich. Whenever a servant of God came to our house, my parents would honor him/her and treat him/her with respect and dignity. If the visit were anywhere near a mealtime, they would make sure that the person did not leave without eating and no one left our home without receiving a "holy handshake."[18]

My parents were amazingly hospitable to anyone who visited us. In fact, as a child, I used to pray for guests to come. Because if guests arrived, we were sure to have exceptional meals!

They also gave to the Lord faithfully. My father would separate the best-yielding coconut tree from among the trees and put a mark of a cross on it. Every coconut harvested from that tree belonged to the Lord. Also, the best of the first fruits from our small farm always went to the church.

Every time my mother cooked rice -which was twice a day-, after measuring the required amount into the cooking vessel, she would take a handful out of that and put it into a special jar.[19] Once that jar was full, it would be taken to the church to be auctioned off to raise funds for the Lord's work.

---

[18] "Holy handshake" is a euphemism for a monetary gift.

[19] This practice is known as "pidi ari" in Malayalam, which means "handful of rice." It was a common practice among believers in Kerala. As money was rare this was a way of giving to the Lord's work among most believers in Kerala. Christians in the Northeastern state of Mizoram

Morning and evening family prayers were regular in our home as it was in most devout Christian homes in our village. Waking up to the sound of beautiful songs rising in the early morning hours was usual for us children. Malayalam, our mother tongue, is rich in its hymnody with many appropriate songs for morning family prayer, evening family prayer, and other occasions. We children learned a lot of Biblical theology just by learning those beautiful songs.

I often heard my grandparents and parents singing hymns and songs throughout the day while they were engaged in everyday life tasks. I can still hear my grandfather singing his favorite Christian song, a famous Malayalam song composed by Sadhu Kochukunju Upadeshi[20] that assures peace amid sufferings. I praise God for such memories.

We, as a family, never missed a Sunday worship service. We had to walk a little over a mile to reach our church. We will all go dressed in our "Sunday best." Every Sunday, we had Sunday School, and attending that was mandatory for us children. The competition was fierce among us children to score the top mark in examinations because we all wanted the first prize. We got a solid foundation in the Bible through Sunday School. We memorized large portions of Scripture.

---

reportedly have raised millions of dollars for Missions through this practice.

[20] Kochukunju Upadeshi (1883-1948) is one of the most well-known preachers in Kerala who, through his preaching, brought a great awakening to the Church in Kerala in the first half of the 20th century. He composed some of the most famous Malayalam Christian songs that are theologically rich and are still regularly sung by Malayali Christians worldwide. Many of his songs were composed amid severe suffering that he experienced, and as a result still serve as a source of comfort and peace to those who go through similar situations in life.

Only once in four weeks, the "Achan"[21] would come to our parish as there were not enough ordained pastors to serve all the congregations. As a result, an ordained pastor would be in charge of several parishes. There would be an evangelist[22] who would take care of limited pastoral duties during the other weeks. But he was not authorized to baptize, serve the Holy Communion, officiate a wedding, or bury the dead.

Another memorable part of our childhood was attending Gospel meetings. Our village was predominantly a Christian village. Most people belonged to CSI, Mar Thoma, or Orthodox churches. And all these churches organized Gospel conventions and prayer meetings regularly. Attending these meetings was exciting for us. Once again, we often had to walk a considerable distance to get to these meetings, which were usually conducted in the evening as people had to work all day on their farms. As I told you earlier, we had no electricity in our village. Torches made with coconut leaves were our "flashlights." A torch made of tightly bound coconut leaves would last a long time as a group of people walked together in its light.

Large crowds would gather for these meetings. Preachers had to speak very loudly since there were no public address systems. Sermons would go on for an hour or two. To protect the preacher's vocal cords, a "repeater" would repeat what the preacher said in a louder voice. The preacher would say one sentence and stop. Then the other person standing beside him would repeat the same sentence louder!

---

[21] Achan is the Malayalam word for an ordained pastor.

[22] He was known as "Upadeshi." An Upadeshi is not qualified for ordination as he did not have sufficient theological training. My father was called an "Upadeshi" by some as he used to help out in the church at times.

Later in my life, after I became a born-again believer, I had the privilege of assisting many preachers as the "repeater." Once I began to preach the Gospel, several people helped me in the same way.

When I was a small baby, my parents dedicated me to pastoral ministry. Though I did not remember that, my mother has often told me that. My father's first cousin, Rev. C. I. Abraham, was a prominent clergyman in the CSI church. As a child, he was my hero. I am told that I would pretend to be him and always say, "When I grow up, I will be Kottayam Appachan Achan."[23] Later, another of my father's first cousins, Rev. George Koshy, was ordained as a clergyman in the CSI church. That added more zeal to my ambition to become an ordained clergyman in the CSI church.

The Chavanikamannil family is an extensive family. My grandfather, Chavanikamannil Chacko Oommen, commonly known as C.C. Oommen, according to our custom, had seven siblings alive when I was a child- four brothers and three sisters. He also had many first cousins. Each of them had several children, grandchildren, and great-grandchildren. He had seven surviving sons and two daughters.[24] My father was the third son. Before I was born, most of the seven sons and their families lived as a joint family.[25] Grandfather had

---

[23] As mentioned above, "Achan" is an ordained clergyman. Rev. C. I. Abraham was the parish priest of the Cathedral Church in Kottayam, the seat of the CSI Bishop. "Appachan" is the term children use to address their fathers or grandfathers.

[24] I say "surviving" because my grandfather and grandmother lost several children in infancy because medical care was indigent, and as a result, infant mortality was very high. I lost two sisters in their infancy.

[25] Joint family system is still practiced by many in India. It is a system where all the siblings and their families live under the same roof. In a time in which families owned a lot of land and agriculture was the only

built a reasonably large house, with room enough for a lot of people. I have heard many fascinating stories of life together with so many people. Let me share just one.

My maternal grandmother was still living when this happened. She was reputed to be a very efficient manager of a large household. In a joint family, all cook and eat together. A system of separate cooking or eating was considered shameful. Daughters-in-law all worked together in cooking and cleaning. Serving the food was the privilege of the grandmother.

Dining tables and chairs were all foreign to our culture. Everyone, except the very elderly, sat on the floor. Some older folks might have a raised wooden seat called "Korandi." My grandfather's house had a large room where everyone sat on the floor and ate. It was a dimly lit room.

Once, my grandfather brought home a very special freshwater fish, famous in our part of the world. It was difficult to get that fish as it was costly and rare. Everyone was eager to eat this fish. It was prepared with special care, and when the time came, my grandmother served it to all, giving equal portions to all the children.

My brother was a small boy of six or seven then. And he had a peculiar habit of eating. He would save what he liked most to eat last, after finishing everything else on his plate. According to that practice, he saved the one piece of fish he got to eat at the very end of his meal.

Everyone had finished their food by the time he was ready to eat his fish. With great anticipation, he bit into the fish. To his utter shock, he discovered that it was not fish at

means of livelihood, this was a very desirable system because many hands were needed to cultivate and take care of the land.

30

all! It was a piece of Malabar tamarind (Malayalam: Kodampuli)![26] As our grandmother's eyesight was failing, she could not distinguish between a piece of fish and kodampuli! By now, all had eaten, and there was no fish left at all. It broke my brother's heart and the heart of our grandmother! The incident made such an impact on everyone that it became a part of the family lore.

In those days, non-vegetarian dishes were luxury for us. It was a special treat to eat fish, chicken, mutton, or beef. And even when we ate any non-vegetarian items, we ate only a small quantity, only as a side dish, never as the main item of the meal as it is in the West. When we had fish, it was dried fish as we had no way to refrigerate items. Fresh fish was a rare treat, and this particular fish was even more seldom. So, you can imagine how terrible a disappointment was for my brother and sorrow for our grandmother.

Education was given very high priority among our people. This was the direct influence of the Church and the Gospel. When Protestant missionaries came to our part of India, education was the exclusive privilege of the so-called "high caste" people. People belonging to the lower castes were allowed to study only rarely, if at all. The so-called "Untouchables" were not at all permitted to learn. It is the Gospel and Christian missionaries that challenged this terribly unjust system.

They established a school with every church and opened it to all, irrespective of religion or caste. When they started schools, there was no word for school in Malayalam. Up to that point education was exclusively the privilege of the "high castes" and teachers were always "high caste" and

---

[26] For Kerala fish curry, Malabar tamarind is an essential ingredient. Once the fish curry is done, it is very easy to mistake a piece of tamarind for fish, especially in low light.

instruction was given in the house of the "guru". So, school was known as *"Guru Kulam"*- meaning, house of the guru. One had to go into the house of the guru to be educated. Who can go into the house of a "high caste" person? Only a member of the "high caste" community! Thus, they effectively barred all so-called "low caste" people from receiving an education.

When missionaries opened schools for all, a new name had to be invented to describe this novel place where everyone was welcome! It is fascinating to learn the name that people coined. It is still the word for school in Malayalam- "Pallikkoodam." What does this word mean? "Palli" is church. "Pallikkoodam" means "building attached to the church!"

This radical concept that education is for all changed the face of Kerala within a few short years. Kerala has the highest literacy rate in all of India because missionaries started schools for all, including women when women were forbidden from learning according to traditional Hindu belief.

We had several schools within walking distance started by Christians. We had no schools nearby started by the majority community. That is a stark statement that shows the drastic difference in worldviews between the Gospel and other faiths.

The Holy Bible teaches that every human being is precious because all are made in the image of God. God loves all equally. That is the declaration of John 3:16, the most famous Bible verse. If every human is made in God's image, every human deserves to study and become all that God intends that person to be. That is the fundamental teaching of the Holy Bible. That's why wherever the Gospel has taken root in India, people's quality of life has improved in terms of all measurable statistics- literacy, life expectancy, and standard of living.

As I said, several schools were started by Christians within walking distance of our house. I first studied in the school in which my father taught. It was hardly half a mile away from our home. It was under the management of a group known as PRDS. But that school became bankrupt when I was in 3rd grade. So, I transferred to the CMS School, Chelakompu, established by CMS missionaries, where Leela was studying. That school was about one mile away. All of us walked to school as none of us even had a bicycle. As stated earlier, our village only had bullock carts.

We had no clocks or watches. Do you know how we told time? We looked at the sun and the shadow! We devised a system to tell time accurately. We would measure the length of our shadows and know what time it was! Oh! How simple life was in those days. We did not need any alarm clocks to wake us up. There were the roosters that would wake us up with their beautiful "alarms."

My father got a wristwatch for the first time when I was about seven or eight. One of my cousins-in-law got a job in the Persian Gulf. When he came home for a vacation, he brought a Swiss-made Favre-Leuba watch for my father. That was big news in our village. Everyone came to see this magical instrument that could tell time! My father was so proud of his precious watch that he kept it safe for many years until I bought him a Seiko watch in 1984!

My mother would pack a lunch and send me off to school. I had a lunch box. But I preferred a lunch packed in banana leaves. There was a unique taste for rice and curry packed in banana leaf! During lunch hour, we would gather around a well to wash our hands and eat lunch. We often would share our lunches among close friends. What a time of joy that was!

I had a devoted cat that would follow me to the boundary of our property when I went to school. There, he would sit on top of a stone hedge and look at me until I disappeared. When I returned from school around four o'clock, he would come and wait at that same place for me to receive me and "take me home". My cat was a good hunter. He loved to hunt chipmunks. He lived for a long time. It was a sad day in our family when that cat died at a ripe old age.

All of us children from the neighborhood walked together to school. We would, at times, fight with each other and soon became intimate friends again. None of us had any footwear. At times, one of us would strike his/her foot against a stone or step on a thornbush, and a thorn would get stuck in the foot. All of us would stop and help that person and make sure s/he could walk again. Several of us in that group are still friends after all these years. I lost my closest friend, V. M. Kurian (Joy), in December 2020 to cancer. He was the same age as me. We studied in the same class through school. How I miss him!

We children had a strange custom among us. A particular shrub grew in plenty on both sides of the mud road that we walked to school. This shrub was known to be a medicinal plant that the villagers used to treat many common ailments. So, we children imagined that it had some magical qualities to it. In Malayalam, it is called "paanal." During certain times of the year, it produced an edible fruit which was beautiful to see and tasted good too.

Corporal punishment was common in those days. Most of our teachers were kind and compassionate; even when they punished us, they did it with restraint and gentleness. Nonetheless, getting corporate punishment was no fun. Our teachers did use canes to punish us!

We children believed that this magical plant had the ability to protect us from receiving spanking from our teachers! How did that work? On the way to school, we would go to a lovely, lush plant and "talk' to it. We will tell the plant that if it would protect us and prevent the teacher from punishing us, we would treat it well when we returned. On the other hand, if we received a spanking from our teacher, then watch out! After this "conversation," we would tie up the poor plant and go to school.

If it was a good day in school and we got no punishment, we will return to the particular bush with which we made the "covenant" and gently untie it and thank it profusely! On the other hand, if we got punished, look out! That was the end of that poor bush. We would destroy it!

Of course, the whole thing was nothing but superstition. But who was going to convince us children of that? We all believed it with all of our heart, mind, soul, and strength, and nobody would convince us that what we were doing was nothing but foolishness. I don't know how this custom got started. But it was a regular part of our journey to school. Looking back at our foolishness convinces me of the veracity of Proverbs 22:15.[27]

Our family was a happy family. It was customary for us children to visit our Aunts and Uncles and sometimes stay with them for days. My father had two sisters, and we loved to go and stay with both of them. Visiting the younger sister was a special joy as her house was near a lovely river. She had four children- two boys and two girls. The oldest was a girl, and she was older than me. The other three were younger than me. We were very fond of each other. They would come and stay with us, and we would go and stay with them often.

When I was about twelve years old, I went to stay with my Aunt for a few days during the summer holidays.

---

[27] "Folly is bound up in the heart of a child,

but the rod of discipline drives it far from him."

Two other cousins, the sons of my father's brother and other sister, also came. Thus, we were seven cousins together, enjoying each other's company. I told my cousins that I wanted to learn to swim. They all knew how to swim well as they grew up near a river. My home was far from a body of water, and I had no opportunity to learn to swim. So, I began to pester my cousins to teach me how to swim. They would take me to the river and try to teach me how to swim. Though they knew how to swim, they did not know how to teach me. After a few attempts, I told them to show me where the deep water was and that I wanted to go to the deep waters. They knew I was nowhere near ready to go to deep waters so pointed to the direction of shallow water and told me that was where the deep water was. Then they all went swimming.

I got cold feet and decided to go to the shallow waters instead. So, I went in the direction my cousins told me was where the shallow water was. Soon, I found myself in really deep water. I was drowning! My cousins saw that I was drowning and began to cry out. One of my cousins, an expert swimmer, tried all he could to rescue me. But he was too small to help me. I was going down. When drowning, once you go down three times, you only come up if someone rescues you. I went down the third time.

Just in the nick of time, hearing the cry of my cousins, a man with a canoe came rushing. He jumped into the water and rescued me before I drowned. God had sent that man just in time. If he were only a few minutes late, I would have drowned and died. God's hand of mercy and grace was upon me, and He sent that man with a canoe just in time to rescue me. This was the second time I was saved from drowning, first in a well and second time in a river.

I can never thank the Lord enough for His grace and mercy. If I had died in that river, I would have ended in eternity apart from God because I did not know Jesus as my personal Savior then, though I was born and raised in a godly home by godly parents. Looking back after six and a half decade, I can say with confidence that He spared my life because He had a plan for my life, a plan to bless me and prosper me, a plan to make me a blessing for many.

As I said before, there were several Gospel conventions all through Kerala. Most famous is the Maramon Convention held on the banks of the Pamba River in Maramon under the auspices of the Mar Thoma Church. It is reputed to be one of the largest Christian gatherings anywhere in the world. It began in 1895 and continues uninterrupted. Another famous convention is the Kumbanad Convention, which is organized by the Indian Pentecostal Church. That began in 1925.

In our village, there was a united convention organized by several churches together. All these spiritual gatherings paved the way for spiritual renewal among the people. Several young people from our village committed their lives to become missionaries in north India and Nepal. Among them is Rev. K.V. Abraham, Leela's first cousin, who became a missionary to Nepal and later to North India. He played a significant role in our lives, as we will see later.

My first cousin and closest neighbor, Mr. C. K. Oommen, became one of the first members of our family to embrace the Pentecostal faith.[28] In those days, Pentecostals were looked down upon by most of us because a significant number of people who became Pentecostals were from the so-called "lower strata" of society. Therefore, it was considered shameful to associate with them. I too was among those who thought that way because I was very proud of our family's Anglican/CMS heritage.

---

[28] The first was my father's first cousin, Pastor C. C. George, who later baptized my brother and me.

At the same time, I greatly respected my cousin, whom I called Thankachayan. He was the first in our family to attend University and earn a degree. And his character was exemplary. So, even though I was prejudiced against Pentecostals, because I respected him, I used to accompany him to prayer meetings held by the Pentecostals.

I attended a prayer meeting with him on November 11, 1961. I was thirteen then. The meeting was in a dilapidated shack. Most people attending were from the so-called "lower strata" of society. Yet, the Holy Spirit's presence in that meeting was powerful. Something shook me deeply in that night's meeting. To this day, I am unable to explain what happened to me there. But I do know that something did happen. I was sobbing all through the evening. My cousin noticed my sobbing and encouraged me to go forward during the altar call. But I was too cowardly to go forward.

When I got back home, I wrote the date in my Bible. That's why I still remember that date. I believe that the Holy Spirit touched me on that day. Yet, I did not yield my life fully to Him. Looking back, I wish I had given myself fully to the Lord that day. I could have avoided several pitfalls in my life had I done that.

Many households in our village subscribed to Malayala Manorama, the oldest daily newspaper in Malayalam. That was our only news source, as radio was unheard of in our village. Even children eagerly waited for the newspaper as there were popular cartoons in it. "Boban and Molly" was very popular with us. The sense of humor of the cartoonist, Mr. Toms, was very appealing to children and adults.

There was also a serial cartoon story called "Mandrake the Magician" in that newspaper. It hooked me. I couldn't wait for the paper to come to find out what happened next in the story! I became enamored with magic through this cartoon series. So, I decided to become a magician. In the same newspaper, there were advertisements promising to teach hypnotism. I somehow earned enough money to enroll in a correspondence course to learn hypnotism. Soon, I received a book and other materials in the mail, and I devoured the material.

I needed subjects to experiment on in the process of learning how to hypnotize people. My little cousins and other children in the neighborhood became my subjects. I was surprised that it was easy to hypnotize most of the children! Soon, my "fame" rose in the neighborhood, and I began to get more volunteers! After a while, I lost interest in it and gave up my ambition to become a magician like Mr. Mandrake!

The newspaper talked a lot about an organization of children they were promoting all over Kerala. It was known in Malayalam as "Bala Jana Sakhyam"- which means the association of children. The newspaper published news and pictures of these associations from all over our state.

I decided that our little village must also have one of these associations. There were a lot of children in our village. Why not gather them together and form an association? I recruited one of my cousins to join me in the venture. We needed to find a place to gather the children together. We found a place hardly a quarter mile away from my home. It was a place used by the Mar Thoma Church to teach Sunday School to local children. It was free on Sunday afternoons. We approached Mr. P.M. Samuel, a respected Christian leader in our village, and asked for his patronage for the association. He was very gracious and agreed to help us. He talked to the people in charge of the "Sunday School Shed," as the "building" was known in the village. It just had four pols holding it up and had no walls. Its roof was thatched by coconut leaves.

We met every Sunday afternoon. Mr. P.M. Samuel would help us to lead the meeting. He would teach us Bible stories and new songs. We children took turns preaching, presenting essays on various topics, singing songs, reciting Scripture verses, and presenting one-act plays. We organized multiple competitions and awarded prizes to the winners. Overall, it was a great experience in organizing and leading. I am sure the Lord was training us for our future ministries through such small things.

By then, my brother was a school teacher at Sacred Heart School, Thevara, Ernakulam (now Kochi), a school under the Carmelite order of Roman Catholic monks. He wanted to ensure that I received a good university education. Because our parents were not financially strong to send him to college when he completed high school, he did not receive a university education. So, he chose to be trained as a crafts teacher and got an appointment at Sacred Heart School.

Later in life, he enrolled in the University and fulfilled his desire to be a graduate. He was a very hard-working person. I would never have received a good education if not for his initiative. He went to be with the Lord on January 24, 2015, at the age of 78. He was a diabetic, as many in our family are.

I am forever grateful to my brother and Kochamma.[29] She treated me like her own brother the eight years I lived with them- 1964 to 1972. I do love my brother and my sister, who, too, went to be with the Lord on June 8, 2018, at the age

---

[29] Kochamma is a term of respect used for several older relatives. As mentioned earlier, our culture demands respect for older people and has many different terms to address them. One of the major culture shocks we experienced when we came to the US was hearing little children calling older people by their first names without any words of respect added!

of 83. I am the only one left. Who knows how long I have left on this earth! However long I have left, my ambition is to live for my Lord, who died for me on the cross of Calvary.

Going to Thevara for a boy raised in a remote village was like going abroad even though it was hardly sixty miles away. My brother had taken me to his place of work a few years earlier. It was the first long trip I took in my life.

We had to walk about two miles carrying our luggage to catch a bus to the nearest boat-jetty in Changanassery. Then we took an overnight boat to Ernakulam. It was my first journey in a boat. For a small boy who had not seen the world outside of his surroundings, all the new sights and sounds were wonderous. My brother treated me to special food and snacks sold in the boat. What special treats those were to a boy who had never eaten restaurant food in his life!

From Ernakulam boat jetty we took another bus to the lodge where my brother was staying with a few other single teachers. All of them treated me with love and care because I was "Oommen sir's baby brother."

My brother's coworkers were competing with each other to make me feel important. They took me to good restaurants and treated me to various dishes I had never even heard of before. I still vividly remember eating "biriyani"[30] for the first time in a restaurant! I didn't even know how to pronounce the word properly. When I came back home, I told

---

[30] There are multiple theories of the origin of biriyani. Most probably, the precursor to it was brought to India by the Turk-Mongol conquerors. Now, the most popular varieties are made with the famous, fragrant "basmati" rice, spices, chicken, mutton, lamb, shrimp, or a combination of several types of meat.

everyone that I ate "piri aani!"[31] And people laughed and looked at me funny!

I remember meeting for the first time the Roman Catholic monks in their coffee-colored cassocks, with the top of their heads shaved. I had never seen a monk before. I had met Catholic priests before in St. John the Baptist Church where we went for the annual festival.

Later many of these monks became my teachers when I enrolled in SH College for my university education. They were dedicated men who committed their lives to serve God as they understood service to God. Some of them were saints and made a deep impact on my life, while there were others who brought shame to God's Name.

---

[31] "Piri aani" in Malayalam means "metal screws"! My friends, who did not know what biriyani was, thought that I was saying that I ate metal screws!

Chapter 2

Leaving Our Little Village
for the Big City.

Photographs were very rare in our childhood. This is the only surviving one of me. Below is Leela as a young girl.

My brother got married in 1962. He lived with his family in a rented apartment about a mile from the school where he taught. Kochamma, his wife, got a job in the Kochi Port Trust.

In those days, high school in our part of the world ended with 10th grade. Every student in the state was given a number and appeared for the final examination of the 10th class at the same time and answered the same questions. Only the number of each student was written on the answer scripts and those were evaluated in a blind system. The result of the 10th grade determined whether one got admission to a good college or not. It was known as the SSLC[32] examination. The results of the examination came in the newspaper!

Leela and I completed 10th in 1964. She was admitted to Mar Thoma College, Thiruvalla, for her Pre-Degree course.[33] My brother took me with him to Ernakulam and got me admission in Sacred Heart College, Thevara. I chose the first group, and she chose the second group.[34] She stayed with her maternal grandparents in Thurithicadu and took a bus to college every day and I lived with my brother and family.

After the two-year Pre-Degree, we had to choose a major for the bachelor's degree. Neither of us chose Science as our major. By then, I had set my sights on becoming a politician for my career and wanted to go to Law School, as most Indian politicians were lawyers. So, I decided on a Philosophy major and sought admission to Maharaja's College, Ernakulam. Leela continued at Mar Thoma College, choosing the double major of Economics and History.

---

[32] Secondary School Leaving Certificate. Passing this examination was considered finishing high school in those days.

[33] As stated earlier, then high school ended with 10th grade. First two years of university education was known as Pre-Degree Class (PDC).

[34] The First group was Physics, Chemistry, and Math; the second group was Physics, Chemistry, and Biology/Zoology; and the third group was History, Economics, and Commerce.

Leela was known as the smartest girl in our village. She was always first in her class and worked very hard, no matter what the task. (Even now, she works hard and cannot rest until all work is done!)

Our houses were in the same village, hardly half a mile apart. Our families have known each other for generations. My first memory of Leela is when she was four or five. We had to walk by her house to go to the market in the main part of our village, known as Noorommavu Junction. Leela's house has a gate to the main road that leads to Noorommavu. She was standing at the gate with her father and some other people. She was very beautiful and buxom, wearing just an underwear, as most little girls in our village used to do then. That memory of her has lived in my heart ever since. I had no idea then that I would be blessed with her hand in marriage. I was way too young to think such thoughts.

In Maharaja's College I became actively involved in students' politics. We are the first free generation of Indians. India became independent in 1947 and I was born in 1948. We grew up keenly aware of the independence struggle and the value of freedom. My father hung the pictures of all major freedom fighters on the wall of our house. We grew up hearing the stories of Mahatma Gandhi, Pandit Jawaharlal Nehru, and all the other giants of the freedom struggle. So, politics was a natural fit for me. And Maharaja's College was the right place to be if one were interested in student politics.

Kerala Students' Union (KSU) was the leading students' political wing of the Indian National Congress, the political party of Gandhi and Nehru. I joined KSU and soon became an active member going for rallies and organizing protests and strikes. A prominent leader of KSU, Mr. Vayalar Ravi, was studying for his M.A. in Maharaja's at that time. His leadership motivated a lot of us young people to work aggressively for the party.

I was slowly drifting away from my Christian convictions and morals and becoming too engrossed in politics. I was fairly good in my studies. The head of the department of Philosophy really liked me and encouraged me to study well. Occasionally, in his lectures, he would challenge us Christians in the class about our faith. As a devout Hindu he was rightly proud of his faith. There were only four Christians in the class- two were Roman Catholic nuns; third, Augustine, was also a Roman Catholic and then the last was me. None of us could defend the Christian faith in any way or give any rational answers to the questions that our professor was raising. Though we were Christians in name, none of us, including the two nuns, knew the Bible well enough to answer the critiques of our professor. That would nag me at times. But then I quickly forgot it and pressed on with my priority- working to promote KSU.

As time went on, I began to take part in violent protests organized by students. One protest march became more violent than we wanted it to become. One of our compatriots was beaten up badly by the police. Some of our friends became angry and destroyed a lot of public property. I was in the thick of all these things. Police took note of me.

It was late at night when I reached home. Being very tired, I fell asleep. By eight or so in the morning, police had traced my address and came looking for me. Kerala police are brutal even today. You can imagine how they were in the 60's. Once they catch you, you will not forget the experience. You would suffer severe consequences to your physical health once they are done with you.

When police came looking for me, I was fast asleep on a bed in the verandah of my brother's apartment. I had not gone to my room since I came home very late the previous night. A shade covered the part of the verandah where the bed was. That shade was relatively thin, and if the policemen had come closer, they would have spotted me. For some reason,

46

they did not come near. They stood a little far and shouted, asking for me by name. The young lady who took care of our household chores, Thanka, went out to them and told them that I had not returned home yet. They turned back and left!

Looking back, that was nothing but the mercy of God. The Lord who blinded the Arameans (2 Kings 6:18) blinded the police officers so that they could not see me, though I was sleeping right in front of them on the porch! Thus, my life was spared a third time by the mercy of God! I deserved to be arrested and beaten up by the police. Since I was a very frail person, a police beating could have been fatal for me. I can only say that God, in His grace and mercy, spared me by making Thanka tell a lie to the police officers. They believed her words and went back.

When my brother understood the seriousness of what I had done, he immediately sent me away to my parents because he knew that if the police caught hold of me that could be my end. I stayed away for over a month until the situation was calm. Student union leaders negotiated with the police and settled all the issues, and the police dropped all the cases. Only then did I return to my brother's place.

I have never liked violence. All that transpired in connection with this protest march that turned violent sowed the first seeds of doubt in my heart about my decision to become a politician. Seeing "big leaders" standing back and pushing naïve students to the front to create violence also sowed the seeds of disillusionment in my heart. Still, I continued the pursuit of that dream of one day becoming a political leader.

Chapter 3

Meeting Jesus and Call to Ministry

In 1967, there was a major war between Israel and the neighboring Arab countries. It is known as the "Six-Day War." Gamal Abdel Nasser, the President of Egypt, declared that he was going to wipe Israel off the face of the earth. The whole Arab world and countries like Iraq and Iran supported the war. Yet, in a surprise attack on June 5th, 1967, Israel destroyed more than 90 percent of Egypt's air force on the tarmac and incapacitated the Syrian air force. When Jordan joined the fight, Israeli forces drove all Jordanian forces out of East Jerusalem in one day. By June 10, 1967, Israel had completely defeated all the countries that threatened them.

As a political junkie, I was utterly engrossed in the news of this war; everyone with any interest in the Arab-Israeli conflict was captivated by the news.

One day, one of my brother's friends came excitedly and told us that a pastor was teaching the Bible nearby and that he was claiming that the Bible has foretold the Six-Day War. That caught our attention. We decided to go to the Bible Study. Pastor P.M. Philip, a well-known Pentecostal pastor, was the teacher. He was a very fascinating personality, and his teaching was captivating.

The main focus of his teaching was on Jesus Christ. Though he taught Bible prophesies about Israel, he would close every study by focusing on Christ. He would repeat a couple of sentences again and again, which made a tremendous impact on me:

"There is no one like Jesus Christ. His biography was written in detail centuries before He was born, and that too not in Christian books, but in Jewish religious books!"

He would point out Scripture after Scripture from the Old Testament books written centuries before the birth of Christ that predicted the coming of the Messiah.

All of a sudden, a thought hit me:

"What this man is teaching can help me to answer my professor. If what he is saying is true, then Jesus is unique. No other religious teacher is like him. I finally have some points to answer my professor".

That motivated me to listen to Pastor Philip carefully. He also taught that the rebirth of Israel in 1948 was part of God's eschatological plan. Israel existed without a land, without a temple, and without a ruler for centuries. No other nation in the history of humanity has survived these many centuries without any of these. He pointed to texts like Deuteronomy 30:3[35], Jeremiah 32:37[36], Ezekiel 34:13 to 37 and 36:24 to 38 that explicitly talk about the scattering and regathering of Israel. We had never heard anyone teaching on these Scriptures. So, we kept going back.

He closed his teaching every night by focusing on Jesus Christ and inviting people to surrender their lives to Christ. The Bible study was for fifteen days. We did not miss a single day. Towards the end of the study, I was fully convinced that the Bible is the Word of God and that Jesus Christ is who the Bible says that He is and that He suffered, died, and rose again to save me from eternal death. I gladly surrendered my life to the Lordship of Christ. And the Lord called me to preach the Gospel. Instantly the Lord took away

---

[35] "…then the LORD your God will restore your fortunes and have mercy on you, and he will gather you again from all the peoples where the LORD your God has scattered you."

[36] "I will restore the fortunes of Judah and the fortunes of Israel, and rebuild them as they were at first.

my desire to be a lawyer and a politician and put in me a passion to preach the Gospel.

At the same time my brother and his wife also gave their lives to the Lord. Though all three of us were raised in godly families, none had confronted us before so powerfully with the need to be born again.

All three of us took water baptism together on October 8, 1967. My father's first cousin, Pastor C. C. George, baptized us along with a few other friends. And on October 13, 1967 Lord blessed me with the baptism of the Holy Spirit.

All my friends immediately noticed a total transformation in me. God gave me great boldness to stand alone and preach the Gospel on our college campus. In the same places where I spoke in political rallies, God gave me the privilege to lift up Jesus. My classmates and friends thought I had become crazy. They laughed at me and called me all kinds of names. But, because of the grace of God, that did not bother me.

We joined the congregation that invited Pastor P.M. Philip to teach the Bible- the Indian Pentecostal Church of Ernakulam. Our pastor was Pastor M.V. Thomas, a man full of zeal for the Lord. He would organize open-air meetings all across the city and ask me to preach. Public speaking did not frighten me because I was used to speaking in political rallies. Though I had no theological training, God gave me grace to be His witness, and a number of people came to know Him through the foolishness of my preaching. Many years later, I have had the blessed privilege of seeing the children of people who met the Lord through my preaching enroll as students in the Bible College/Seminary we pioneered.

Pastor Thomas discipled us and taught us to serve the Lord wholeheartedly. We must do anything we do for the Lord with all of our being. That early training has helped me understand that ministry is not just preaching or teaching from behind a pulpit. Ministry is one's whole life. It is *being and not just doing.* Cleaning the church and arranging seats for people to sit is just as important as preaching and teaching. The Lord honors and rewards all who do even the tasks that some people might consider unimportant. God gave me the grace to take my pastor's teaching to heart, and I did not hesitate to do anything that needed to be done.

Later, when our church had enough money to purchase a PA system, we would carry it to places where we conducted Gospel meetings. Climbing trees to hang the speaker became one of my favorite tasks as it was easy because I was very slim and tall!

God gave me the courage to stand alone in crowded street corners to preach the Gospel. Whenever I went home to my parents, I would encourage my childhood friends to go with me to preach the Gospel. Most would refuse because people would make fun of Gospel preachers, even in our village, which was predominantly Christian, at least in name. Then, I would ask my nephew Babu, whose formal name is George C. Kuruvilla, ten years younger than me, to accompany me. Though a child, he would come with me, and we would go and preach wherever we could get a few people to listen to us. Years later, the Lord would make him a missionary to North India. When the Lord called us back to India to pioneer a work in North India, he became our righthand person.

Miraculously, almost the same time that we came to the Lord, God was speaking to our only sister and her husband, though they were far away from us. Our brother-in-law, Mr. P.C. Kuruvilla, was a senior police officer in Andaman and Nicobar Islands, five hours by flight from

51

where we were, and our sister was in her home about sixty miles away. Our brother-in-law had no intention of serving the Lord. He, a chain smoker, was a military man all his life and had resisted the call of God all his life. His mother and older sister were profoundly spiritual and were crying out to the Lord for his salvation. God heard their cries and saw their tears and called him to Himself, and he took baptism in Andamans. At almost the same time, our sister also followed Christ and yielded her life to Him.

Our parents were at first not very happy with our decision to take baptism as they had baptized us in the Anglican/CMS church as infants. Moreover, as stated earlier, our family was prominent in the Anglican/CMS community, and Pentecostals were looked down upon by most in that circle. Later, they understood that our path was pleasing to God, and in their old age, they, too, decided to obey the Lord in baptism. Our maternal grandmother took baptism when she was 80 plus!

Chapter 4

Falling in Love

I graduated with my BA in 1969. Since I dropped the plan to become a lawyer, I decided to pursue an MA in English language and literature. While studying for my MA, God blessed me with opportunities to travel to many parts of Kerala and preach in small and large Gospel Conventions.

Leela also graduated with her BA degree in 1969. As mentioned, her cousin, Rev. K.V. Abraham, was a missionary in Kathmandu, Nepal. He informed her that school teachers were needed in Nepal, and if she were interested, he could arrange for her to get a job as a teacher there. She jumped at the prospect and left for Nepal right after graduation. She got a teaching job in a small private school when she reached Kathmandu. A few months later, she got an appointment as a teacher in the best school in Kathmandu, the prestigious Saint Mary's Convent School.

Since I had abandoned my plans to become a lawyer and enter politics, I decided to continue my University education. I joined Sacred Heart College for my M.A. in English Language and Literature as there was no master's degree course available in Philosophy in our city then. If that opportunity had been open, I would have pursued my further studies in philosophy as I thoroughly enjoyed the study of philosophy.

It turned out that I enjoyed English literature just as much or even more than Philosophy. There were some excellent professors in the English department of Sacred Heart College in those days. Milton, Shakespeare, Wordsworth, Shelley, and many other English writers became dear to me.

Along with my studies, I continued my preaching as the Lord kept opening doors for me to preach in small and large Gospel conventions. I was blessed with the privilege of preaching the Gospel and marveled at the grace of God that He would use such a person as me to proclaim His Word. One invitation to preach at a large convention in a place called Valakam really surprised me. Only very prominent and seasoned preachers preached at that convention, as it was a large and famous gathering. I was hardly 21 and not at all a "prominent" preacher.

Pastor K. E. Abraham, the most well-known Pentecostal preacher in our part of the world, was scheduled to preach there. He became ill and could not go. So, he called the convention organizers and told them to invite me in his place. I was amazed when I heard Pastor Abraham requested that I speak in his place! I had no idea that he had even heard of me. That was an undeserved honor for a young preacher. God, in His grace, used me very powerfully in that convention. That opened up more invitations to preach, and I became a fairly well-known evangelist in Kerala. God's ways are unique and mysterious indeed!

When I completed my MA, I got a job teaching English in a "Tutorial College" called Wisdom College in Ernakulam. Tutorial colleges are private colleges that coach students who did not gain admission to a college affiliated to a University. They were allowed to appear for University examinations as private students. These institutions also help students who fail their university examinations to appear again.

I thoroughly enjoyed teaching. Soon, I became one of the most popular teachers in Wisdom College, and students clamored to be in my class. The college's principal was pleased with me and publicly commended me many times. I thought I had found my niche. Yet, deep within me, I knew I was not where God wanted me. I planned to work to earn my living and preach part-time. I had forgotten that I had a call on my life; I was living in disobedience because I liked the money I made! How quickly can the evil one deceive us through money?

My starting salary was Rupees 500 (roughly $100 according to the exchange rate of 1971) per month, which was not bad for a 23-year-old single man. When I got paid the first month's salary, I went to my pastor and gave him the tithe before I spent any money on myself. We have always tried to practice that in our lives. And God has honored us for that. God's Word is infallible. When we honor God with our tithes and offerings, He blesses us just as His Word promises. If you want to see God open the windows of heaven and bless you, obey God's Word. Sadly, so many people live in disobedience in money matters and expect to see God's blessings in their lives. *Faith is obedience, and obedience is faith.*

During the summer holidays of 1971, Leela came on vacation from Nepal with Miss Bell, an older British lady who was her colleague and housemate. I was thrilled to have the opportunity to be their "tour guide" as they visited Ernakulam and Kochi. Leela's younger brother, Rajan, also accompanied them during the visit.

As noted earlier, I admired Leela for her brilliance and was attracted to her as she was a very vibrant and beautiful young lady. I had no idea how she felt towards me as our culture did not allow young people to "date" or have any close contact. Because of that, we had never spent time together, even though we were neighbors. For the first time in our lives, Miss Bell's visit allowed us to be close to each other and spend time talking with one another for a few days.

They stayed in a hotel in the city, and I would take them to all the tourist spots from early morning to evening.

As it was summer vacation, I was free, and I made sure not to have any preaching assignments during the days of their visit.

I had no idea whether Leela had any feelings for me. As the last day of their tour approached, I decided that I better find out how she felt about me before they left. I was scared. I had all kinds of fears in my heart. What if she rejects me? Maybe she has someone else? Such thoughts troubled me very much. That night, I spent considerable time in prayer, seeking God's will. The following day, when we met, I mustered up enough courage and diplomatically broached the subject. To my utter and pleasant surprise, I discovered she had feelings for me, too! What a joyous moment that was!

Our love for one another grew strong swiftly. After our time together with Miss Bell, we began to write letters regularly to each other. In those days, letter-writing was the only way to stay in touch as we had no access to a telephone. Of course, there was no email then. I cherished every letter she sent me and wrote even before I got a reply. Photographs were a great help. I kept several photos as bookmarks to see her even when I taught in college!

I had a significant advantage in wooing her: her parents liked me! In our culture, if the parents do not approve of a man or a woman, it would be tough for a marriage to take place. Leela's father liked my preaching, and her mother was fond of me. That was a great advantage and allowed me to spend as much time with her whenever she came home from Nepal.

I continued teaching at Wisdom College and, at the same time, kept busy with my preaching ministry. As stated above, I knew deep within that I was living in disobedience even though I tried to justify my disobedience by saying to God that I was preaching His Word every weekend! How we find ways to justify our disobedience is indeed very comical!

Slowly, God, in his grace, made my life miserable in Wisdom College. The Principal, who liked me and used to compliment my teaching profusely, turned against me. Even though I enjoyed teaching and students loved my teaching, I knew that God was telling me to leave. I have learned from experience that God does speak through circumstances. So, I submitted my resignation after one year of teaching.

My cousin, Rev. C. George, pioneered the ministry of Every Home Crusade (EHC)[37] in Kerala in the 1960s. He was serving as the Principal of the Teachers' Training College in Kottayam, Kerala, when the Lord asked him to resign from his prestigious job and venture into a faith journey with EHC. He quit his teaching career in 1964 and started working with EHC.

He asked me to join him to help with translation work and outreach ministries on college campuses. So, as soon as I left Wisdom College in 1972, I joined the staff of EHC's office in Kottayam and took up the responsibility of translating material from English to Malayalam and organizing outreach ministries to all the college campuses in and around Kottayam. Thus, I entered full-time Christian ministry at the age of 24.

God began to open even more doors for preaching once I moved to Kottayam. Pastor M.T. Joseph, a man with a burning heart for the Gospel, befriended me and took me around to preach all around Kottayam and neighboring towns and villages. Through him, I met several prominent Christian leaders, and all of them encouraged me in the ministry. I spoke in many large and small Gospel rallies and, God in His

---

[37] Every Home Crusade is a ministry pioneered by a Canadian pastor, Jack McAlister. He founded the World Literature Crusade in 1952 with the goal of placing a piece of Gospel literature in every home. The ministry is now called Every Home for Christ.

grace, opened the hearts of scores of people to receive the message and believe in the Lord Jesus Christ.

In those days, there was a growing movement of "rationalists" in Kerala. These were atheists who were making fun of Christians and other people of faith using science as a cover. Though I had no training in apologetics, God gave me the grace to debate with them and expose the shallowness of their arguments. That made me very popular with young people, especially university students. Many would walk for miles to come and hear me preach! Well, God used a donkey once to speak to a man. I have no difficulty believing that. If he could speak through me, He could indeed speak through a donkey!

Chapter 5

Off to Minneapolis!

In the meantime, God, in His own way, was unfolding His plan to use the two of us for His glory. Among the students in Kerala, there was a common custom. Before we graduate and say goodbye to our friends, we exchange our addresses in a small book called "Autograph." All would write some kind of comments, usually humorous, and then write his/her address. This gave us a means to stay in touch with our friends with whom we wanted to keep in touch. Like all others in her class, Leela also had an "Autograph."

One fine morning, a letter from one of her classmates arrived at her home. Leela's father mailed that letter to her in Kathmandu unopened. The gist of the letter was as follows: he had applied to a Bible College in Minneapolis. For some reason, he was not admitted. He thought that, since Leela was the brightest student in their class, she might get admission. He wanted her to have the address if she were interested in applying!

Why he would write such a letter to Leela baffled all of us. She immediately contacted her parents and me and asked our opinion. We all thought it was a great idea as I wanted to equip myself for ministry. I was preaching regularly with no theological training. If God opens the door to the US for Leela, I can follow her and study His Word. So, why not give it a try?

So, Leela wrote a letter to North Central Bible College, Minneapolis, Minnesota, in late 1971. She did not give it much thought as she continued her teaching. We all prayed and asked the Lord to open that door only if it was His perfect will.

In a few months, an admission letter came with all the necessary papers to apply for a J1 visa to the United States. She went to the United States Embassy in Kathmandu and dropped off the application and passport one morning. They told her to come back in the afternoon. When she went back, the visa was ready!

Slowly, excitement was building in all of us. No one from our little village had gone to the United States. We knew that some very prominent people, like Pastor K.E. Abraham, the founder of the Indian Pentecostal Church, have visited the US. Their travel was so newsworthy that the major Malayalam newspaper, Malayala Manorama, would report it! Now a 23-year-old girl from our village was going to America! The whole village was excited!

Nonetheless, Leela was deathly afraid. She did not know a soul in that faraway country. Where will she live? Where will she get the money to pay her fees or buy food? All kinds of questions rushed through her, and there were no easy answers. In those days, the government of India would permit a person who travel abroad to take only $7 (US) out of the country! That added to her anxiety.

During a prayer meeting organized to pray for her just before she began her journey, someone told her about a young man who went to America. He was washing dishes in a restaurant for his living! When she heard that, her fear and anxiety multiplied. She was leaving a good job as a teacher in a prestigious Convent school, and she might have to wash dishes to make a living!

But she thought that no one else, including her parents or I, seemed to care about her fears as we were excited about her going to America!

On the day of her journey, August 31, 1972, her parents and several other relatives took a train to Kochi from where she was to catch her flight to Bombay (now known as Mumbai). I met them at the railway station. We took a taxi to the airport. The taxi dropped us off at the airport. In our excitement and hurry, we forgot to take her luggage out of the cab! And the driver left!

Total panic! How is she going to the US with just the clothes on her back? She had nothing else. A few influential friends who were with us made urgent phone calls to the police and sought their help to locate the taxi. We were all praying fervently for a supernatural intervention. Kochi is a large city with hundreds, if not thousands, of taxis. How will we locate this taxi before the flight takes off?

God answered our prayers. Just in time, somehow, the police contacted the taxi driver, and he came with the luggage, profusely apologizing. And Leela flew to Bombay and got her connecting flight to New York.

But troubles were not over yet! Air India flight from Bombay to New York was late. When it landed at JFK, the last flight to Minneapolis had left! Here is a young lady stuck in New York airport overnight who has never traveled internationally. The airline was gracious enough to provide a hotel room. She could not sleep a wink in that strange place. Fear and worry kept her awake most of the night. The following day, the hotel shuttle took her back to JFK, and she caught her flight to Minneapolis.

She landed in Minneapolis on September 1, 1972, with $7 in her purse. North Central Bible College was expecting her the previous night and had sent a student to receive her and take her to the college. She could not contact the college and inform them of her new arrival flight information. So, there was no one to receive her there!

After collecting her luggage, she went to the taxi stand, showed the driver the address (910 Elliot Ave. S.), and asked him how much it would cost to get there. To her utter relief, the driver said, $6.50! Thus, Leela reached North Central Bible College with fifty cents in her purse to begin life in America.

Looking back, how can we not thank the Lord a billion times, a trillion times, and even more for His grace, mercy, providence, and provisions?

The college assigned her a dormitory room with two godly female students: Ann Michaelson and Beverly Clements. Soon, she got a bill for $620! That was just for the tuition and room. Food was not included! Where is she going to get this much money? Where will she get money to buy food? Her roommates graciously helped her with food and other necessities.

North Central Bible College had a very godly and gracious Dean in those days: Dean Nelson. Leela went to him and told him that she got this huge bill and she had no money to pay. He consoled her and assured her that the college would find her a job and that she only needed to pay the bill in installments when she got paid.

Within a day, she got a job with the Billy Graham Evangelistic Association. Her salary was $1.80 an hour. She attended classes from 8 to 1 and went to work from 3 to 11. She often had to walk about three miles to work and got a ride back to the dorm with some other students. Being a brilliant student, she found her studies fairly easy. She was studying for her Master's degree in Kathmandu, and NCBC offered only a bachelor's degree in those days.

We continued our letter-writing campaign from opposite sides of the globe as telephone connection from the US to Kerala was impossible in those days. I stayed up one night expecting a call from her to our office phone; she tried her best to call but never got a connection. So, we kept writing letters. We both kept praying for the Lord's time for us to be united again.

One day, Dean Nelson called Leela to his office and asked her whether there was anyone she wanted to bring to NCBC. She jumped at the opportunity and said that there was a person. Soon, Dean Nelson sent all the necessary papers for my visa.

My brother and I traveled to Madras (now Chennai) to the US Consulate. Chennai office was notorious for denying visa applications. We went with prayer. The officer who interviewed me hardly asked any questions. From his comments, I felt he liked the name Kuruvilla. Could it be that he had a friend with that name? Anyway, he granted me a J1 visa that afternoon. The thought that I was one step closer to seeing my beloved elated me beyond description.

Soon, we made all the preparations, and I was off to Minneapolis on August 8, 1973, a little less than a year after we sent Leela off. It was the first time I had ever seen the inside of an airplane. When we were in primary school classes, if the teacher heard the noise of an aircraft flying way high in the sky, she would take the entire class outside and point to the sky for us to see an airplane flying! In those days, we never dreamed that we would see an airplane up close, let alone fly in one. How times have changed!

On the flight to Bombay, I sat next to a Bishop from the Orthodox church. He was a very gracious and kind person. He recognized that this was my maiden flight and helped me buckle the seat belt and put cotton in my ear.

From Bombay, I flew Trans World Airlines (TWA). The first stop was in Tel Aviv. I longed to get down in the land where the Lord Jesus walked. But, due to the prevailing tensions there, we were not permitted to leave the aircraft. Years later, God fulfilled my desire to walk where the Lord walked, the land I first saw in 1973 through an airplane window.

From Tel Aviv, we flew to Rome. We had to wait several hours for our connecting flight to New York. The sights and sounds of the Rome airport were all new to me. In Rome airport, I saw one of the first "strange" sights in the Western world that puzzled me- white ladies whose legs were black! I was utterly perplexed by that sight! How could this be? How can people have two colors in their body? Only much later did I learn that these ladies were wearing black pantyhoses and that they were not multi-colored creatures!

I needed to use the restroom in the airport as the wait there was for a few hours. I was again shocked by another "strange" Western custom: I had to pay to use the bathroom! I only had $7, just like Leela when she traveled. It cost me fifty cents to use the toilet! You talk about shock!

Later in the day, on August 8, 1973, I landed in New York, JFK, in time for my connecting flight to Minneapolis. Leela was there with several people in Minneapolis airport to receive me, unlike when she landed there on September 1, 1972. Since she was already in the US, I faced comparatively minimal difficulties.

There were several Malayali families in Minneapolis that Leela had already befriended. One of those families, Mr. and Mrs. Immanuel Abraham, welcomed me into their home, an apartment within walking distance of NCBC. Their little son, Santhosh, was delighted to have me in his home.

Mrs. Abraham, whom I called Mary Ammamma,[38], was very gracious and kind, making me feel at home in the new world.

I completed the registration process in NCBC, and just like Leela, I got a big bill in my hand! Since she had already explained to me the process, I did not panic as she did a year ago! Then, we walked to the Social Security office. Another surprise was waiting for me there.

Earlier, I talked about the system of naming children in the Syrian Christian community and how my name was changed from Kuruvilla C. George to George Kuruvila C. by the Principal of the first school I was enrolled in. (See footnote #7).[39] I wrote my name as George C. Kuruvila when I applied for a Social Security number. The person in charge looked at me and said: "According to your passport and visa, that's not your name. Your name is George Kuruvila Chavanikamannil. You must write it as it is in the visa and passport."[40]. Thus, my name in the US became George K Chavanikamannil.[41]

---

[38] As stated earlier, our culture does not address older people by just their names. A word of respect must be added to his/her name. "Ammamma" is such a word used to address older women.

[39] The Principal had made two changes. He not only changed the order of my name but also the spelling of my name. I always spelled Kuruvilla with two "l." He dropped one "l" and made it Kuruvila. In India, even now, we see many humorous examples of teachers altering children's names. The parents of a young man who studied at New Theological College had named him Daniel, but his school Principal wrote in the TC his name as "Denial!" He is now stuck with his name as Denial!

[40] Looking back, I can say with confidence that even this "mistake" was according to the Lord's plan. Years later, when the Lord called us to go to North India to serve the Lord, the first person to join with us to help pioneer the work, is my nephew, my sister's second son, who according to our custom was named after my father, George. His official name is George C. Kuruvilla. Imagine all the confusion it would have created if I

Even before I arrived in the US, we had set our wedding date as September 1, 1973, just a few days after my arrival. Leela had become a member of Jackson Street Assembly of God Church in St. Paul. The pastors were very gracious and helpful to her. They called her "Lilly." They also received me with warm Christian love and helped us immensely.

As we both had very little money, our wedding was planned as a very simple wedding. Of course, none of our family members could attend our marriage. We were sad about that. And yet, September 1, 1973, is the best day of our lives when the Lord united us as husband and wife.

Pastor K. K. John, then Director of Assemblies of God Campus Ministries, solemnized our marriage. An elderly member of our church, Mr. Promili, walked Leela down the aisle and "gave her away" to be married, as her father or anyone else from the family could not be there.

---

too were George C. Kuruvilla! Lord knew that we would be working together and changed my name to Chavanikamannil, even though it is a very hard name to pronounce for most of our friends from the West. When our first-born, Finny, became a medical doctor, because of the difficulty in pronouncing Chavanikamannil, he changed his name to Dr. Finny George Kuruvilla! Our younger son also has formally changed his name to Renny George Kuruvilla. Circle is complete!

[41] Chavanikamannil is our actual family name. Most Syrian Christians keep their family name only as an initial.

The newly married couple with Dean Nelson

Leela's roommates, Ann and Beverly, helped us so much. With the help of our pastors and several church members, they organized the reception. It was a very simple reception with punch, nuts, and sandwiches.

Our friend, Lazaro Uribe, volunteered to take photographs. The sad part of that story is that his camera malfunctioned, and we lost all the pictures! So, we have no wedding pictures except for a few snaps that some other friends took. Of course, Lazaro felt terrible. But there was nothing anyone could do. As the old saying goes, there is no point in crying over spilled milk. We were so glad that God did many miracles for us and united us in holy matrimony that the absence of pictures did not bother us so much.

We had no money for a honeymoon. The International Students' Ministry Director in Minneapolis graciously gave us a room in her beautiful home in Minnetonka. It was a lovely home. While we were there, snow fell for the first time that year. I had never seen snow before in my life. It was a wonderful sight for me, and so very beautiful. I ran outside and played in the snow like a little child.

We had rented a studio apartment owned by NCBC. It was next door to the college. We began our married life in that tiny apartment, with just one room with a tiny kitchen and a bathroom. But it was a palace for us. We hardly had any vessels to cook. We used an old coffee percolator someone gave us to cook rice and even made curry in it! It was all an adventure for us. As we were in love, none of these difficulties bothered us much.

NCBC gave us many wonderful friends. Mike and Mona Shields are among them. They are a wonderful missionary couple serving the Lord with Assemblies of God in South America. Mike worked with the North Western Bank computer center on Hennepin Avenue in downtown Minneapolis. As he was planning to quit his job, he took me to his boss and recommended me as a replacement for him. Thus, I got my first job in the US. My shift was from 4 PM to midnight. I was assigned to operate a check-sorting machine. It was not a difficult job, so I picked it up rather quickly. The work environment was pleasant and friendly.

We were full-time students at NCBC, and our daily schedule was rather demanding. The morning chapel service was at 8 AM, and then classes till 1 PM. We would rush home, prepare lunch, and then go to work. Leela's shift started at 3 PM. I would walk with her to the Billy Graham Evangelistic Association offices where she worked. From there, I would walk to the North Western Bank administrative building for my work.

In those days, there were no buses in Minneapolis after 10 PM. So, my only option to get home was to walk when my shift ended at midnight. Our apartment was about three miles away. Once winter became severe, walking three miles in the middle of the night became very challenging. I was skinny in those days and had no natural "insulation" in my body. Minnesota winter went right through my body! I tried to put on as many layers of clothes as possible. Nothing seemed to help! I can still remember feeling like a thousand needles being driven through my toes and nose!

Some days, the snow drift would pile up so much snow in front of our little apartment that we could not open our front door. We had to call friends to come and move the snow before we could open the door and get out.

At first, I did not know how to walk on snow and ice and fell often. Once, I fell as I was walking with two bags of groceries and broke all the eggs we had bought.

We started praying for a baby. In preparation for a baby, we decided to get adequate health insurance and signed up with Blue Cross and Blue Shield. Since we were both full-time students and our tuition bill was expensive, paying for insurance was difficult. So, I decided to take a weekend job in addition to my job with North Western Bank. I got a job as a janitor in a nursing home through a friend.

Though we were not rich people in Kerala, none in our family had ever done such work. In our culture, janitors were almost always from the so-called "untouchable" caste.[42]

---

[42] "Traditionally, the groups characterized as untouchable were those whose occupations and habits of life involved ritually polluting activities, of which the most important were (1) taking life for a living, a category that included, for example, fishermen, (2) killing or disposing of dead cattle or working with their hides for a living, (3) pursuing activities that brought the participant into contact with emissions of the human body, such as feces, urine, sweat, and spittle, a category that included such occupational groups as sweepers and laundry workers, and (4) eating the

If my parents, relatives or friends knew what a "janitor" was, they would have been really shocked that I was working as one.

One of the greatness of America is that such prejudices have not taken root here and that all work has dignity. The horribly evil concept of caste system developed in India centuries ago based on at least two main factors: color of the skin and nature of work. All those who did the so-called "unclean" work were condemned as "unclean" and, therefore, as "untouchables." Even today, many from the so-called "high caste" will not in any way associate with an "untouchable."

I was in for some major culture shocks in my work as a janitor in that nursing home. My boss was a cruel man. He mistreated me a lot. He hardly would do any work and made me do his work also. I put up with him because I needed the money and I did not mind hard work.

What bothered me most was the condition of the elderly in that nursing home. Several of them, both men and women, would stop me and talk to me and complain about their children not coming to see them. I still vividly remember a very elderly gentleman who was frail and unable to get up stopping me every time I went into his room. With tears in his eyes he would ask me: *"Can you please call my son and tell him to come and see me? He doesn't come to see me."* Of course, I was helpless and could not do anything for

---

flesh of cattle or of domestic pigs and chickens, a category into which most of the <u>indigenous</u> tribes of India fell." Britanica.com accessed on February 9, 2021.

him. It broke my heart that parents who worked hard to raise their children are lonely in their old age. I had no idea about that side of the American life and it really shook me.

In India, we were taught to respect, actually revere, and take care of the elderly. As I stated earlier, my parents took real good care of our grandfather and grandmother. Here, in this land of the plenty, these elderly people were telling me that they were unwanted by their children.

I can never forget the faces and sounds of those dear people in that nursing home. It opened for me a window of the American life of which I was totally ignorant.

I know this is a very difficult issue. Children have their own lives and they are extremely busy. Caring for elderly parents, once they become unable to care for themselves, is a very challenging conundrum. Praise God for the millions of caring people who care for their elderly parents and grandparents with love and compassion in spite of all difficulties. Leela and I met several such people later on, and that helped us to change our perspective.

In our early married life, we were broke. We made just enough money to pay our tuition fees, rent, and buy groceries. Our big treat was on paydays. Leela and I would walk to the McDonalds on Hennepin Avenue, downtown Minneapolis, and eat lunch there: big Mac, French fries, and Coca-Cola, and top it off with hot apple pie! What a treat that was! We are truly grateful to the Lord for His provisions.

One Sunday evening, Leela craved ice cream. We had just enough money to buy an ice cream cone from Dairy Queen. So, hand-in-hand we walked to the nearest Dairy Queen. Elliot Park was right in front of NCBC. In those days, during weekends the park would be frequented by a number of Native Americans. Most of them would be drunk and sometimes they would harass passersby. We had to walk by that park to get to the Dairy Queen. We were very careful to avoid the drunks as we were really afraid of them. There was a tall hedge that separated the park from the sidewalk of 11th Avenue South. There were several breaks in the hedge through which people could enter or exit the park. We were walking on the sidewalk, being careful to avoid any drunks that might come from the park.

All of a sudden, a gentleman stepped right in front of us from the park through one of the openings in the hedge. In an instant, that person put his hand forward to shake my hand. Instinctively I stretched my hand forward to respond to him. He shook my hands, left something in my hand, and walked past us just as quickly as he appeared. By the time I opened my hand and looked to see what he had put in my hand and turned to say "thank you," the person had disappeared, probably back into the park through one of the openings in the hedge.

There was a twenty-dollar bill in my hand! Twenty dollars was a lot of money for us in 1973. A week's grocery hardly cost us ten dollars. We were on the way to spend the last coin we had. God who knew that had sent an "angel" with twenty dollars for us. No human knew that we had no money, but our Lord knew.

Most would discard such incidents as "pure coincidence." But we know better! Our God is the sovereign Lord who takes care of every bird in the air and every grass in the field and He cares for His children. He knows what our needs are even before we know them, and He makes provisions for us. In those days of financial difficulties, we learned to trust the Lord. He was preparing us to trust Him for greater things.

A few months after we got married, we faced a major crisis in our lives. The Immigration and Naturalization Services (INS) of the United States government started an inquiry of North Central Bible College. The inquiry found a number of violations of INS regulations in the way in which NCBC was issuing visa papers to foreign students. So, INS suspended NCBC's authorization to bring and retain foreign students. All of us students were given two options: either return to our home countries or find educational institutions that would admit us and issue proper visa papers.

When the news arrived, all of us international students were shocked. Once again, looking back, we can say with certainty that it was the Lord's hand moving. Events such as these have confirmed our conviction that Romans 8:28 is indeed the absolute truth: *"And we know that in all things God works for the good of those who love him, who have been called according to his purpose."*

I already had my master's degree from the University of Kerala. NCBC offered only a bachelor's degree in those days (Now it is a University that offers advanced degrees). If such a situation did not arise, we might have been happy to stick around NCBC for a few more years and that would have been not very productive for us in terms of ministerial development. The Lord knew it and he was shaking our nest like an eagle does to teach its eaglets to fly!

I had a desire to study at Fuller Theological Seminary. Because of the famous missionary to India, Dr. Donald McGavran, who founded the School of World Missions at Fuller Seminary, many have heard of the school in India.

When this option of going to another school that would issue a J1 visa was presented to us, we immediately checked with Fuller and found that the school did issue J1 visa.

Leela decided that she did not want to study anymore and that she would work and support my theological education. So, immediately we applied to Fuller for admission for me and decided to seek a dependent J2 visa for Leela. By God's grace, I got admission to Fuller Seminary, and we decided to move to Pasadena, California, to start classes in September 1974.

The investigation of NCBC was headed by an INS officer, Mr. Mark Stauffer. In the process of investigating the college, he interviewed several students, including us. We were all deathly afraid to even hear the names Mr. Stauffer and INS!

At the time of this crisis, in June 1974, we discovered that we were pregnant with our first baby. We immediately wrote to our parents and informed them of the exciting news. We had no way of calling them and talking to them in those days. It took a week to ten days for our letter to reach them and another week or ten days for their reply to reach us! How times have changed, and communication has become instant!

With her pregnancy, it became difficult for Leela to continue her work with Billy Graham Ministries. So, she resigned her job. Our dear friend, Ann Michaelson, was working in a hospital near NCBC. She helped Leela to get a job there as an aide to the dietitian.

In August 1974 we got a phone call from Mr. Stauffer. Leela took the call. She was shocked by the call. Mr. Stauffer wanted to come to our home for lunch before we left for California! We had never heard of INS officers making such requests to any foreign students. When Leela told him that we would be honored to have him, he made another request: "May I bring my wife with me?" Leela was wondering what this man was up to. "Please bring her," she replied.

Mr. and Mrs. Stauffer showed up in our small, one room apartment on the appointed day. We tried our best to make the apartment look its best. We hardly had any good furniture. These are VIPs and we wanted to please them as much as we could. They seemed genuinely happy to be visiting with us.

After a few words of greetings, Mr. Stauffer pulled out an envelope from his pocket, handed it to us, and asked us to open it. When we opened the envelope, we were surprised to find papers stamped with a J1 visa for me and a J2 visa for Leela. We did not know what to say.

As we were shocked and overjoyed and were fumbling for words to thank him, he told Leela: *"Look on the other side of your visa."* She turned over the paper. We could not believe our eyes! There it was stamped: *"Employment Authorized."*

Mr. Stauffer went on to say: *"You are going to Los Angeles. It is a very big city, and the INS department there is very large. It might not be easy for you to apply there and get authorization to work. So, I thought I will help you by giving you permission to work."*

We could not believe our eyes or ears. Here was the man who caused so many difficulties for NCBC and all the foreign students, including us, granting us permission to work without us even applying for it! Our God is indeed good!

We thanked him profusely. We were so glad that Leela said "yes" when Mr. Stauffer called and wanted to come and have lunch with us even though, at first, we did feel resentment toward him for all the trouble he unleashed for so many people and for NCBC. Once again, God was teaching us the veracity of Romans 8:28.

We know it was the Lord who moved in the heart of Mr. Stauffer. He knew that we were going to the most expensive seminary in the US and without a work permit for Leela, we would not be able to make it.

Chapter 6

Adventure of Faith
in the Golden State

Our friends in Minneapolis gave us a loving "send-off" with prayer and blessings. They helped us pack all our belongings into a couple of suitcases, and we were off to Los Angeles, California.

We flew North-Western Airlines, and our flight was to land around 9 PM in LAX. We began to see the lights of the vast city of Los Angeles long before landing. We could not believe our eyes! "How large is this place," we wondered aloud. Leela turned to me and asked me, "*How will we find a place to live in this place? It is so big!*" Yet, we knew deep within our hearts that the Lord who called us would undoubtedly take care of us.

Darwin Michaelson, brother of Anne, Leela's roommate in NCBC, met us at Los Angeles airport and took us to a lovely home belonging to one of their relatives. We stayed with that family for a day. The next day, Rev. Ray Stamps, a Fuller student, met us and took us to his home. His wife, Linda, and their lovely little daughter, Charis, hosted us graciously. We can never forget their Christian love and hospitality.

Billy Graham was conducting a Crusade in the Hollywood Bowl the following week. We had an invitation to attend the special seminar for Christian leaders that the Billy Graham Evangelistic Association (BGEA) had organized in the Hollywood Presbyterian Church. BGEA gave us a room in the Hollywood Roosevelt Hotel, right in the heart of Hollywood, and a bus would take us to and from the seminar during the daytime and the Hollywood Bowl in the evening when Dr. Graham preached. Hearing many eminent speakers during the workshop and then listening to Billy Graham preach at night was a blessed privilege. It was a memorable way to begin our theological training at Fuller Seminary! God arranged everything perfectly as only He can.

After the BGEA meetings, we moved into an apartment belonging to Fuller Seminary. The tuition and rent bills were so huge that they depleted all our savings, except for a bit of money we had set aside for the expenses related to our baby's arrival, which was due in February 1975. So, we needed to seek a job for Leela immediately.

Since we did not have a car, the job had to be within walking distance. Because of the few months of experience Leela working as an aide in the hospital's dietary department in Minneapolis, we decided to look for a hospital and apply for a similar job. Someone told us about Huntington Memorial Hospital and gave us directions to get there. After walking for a while, we became frustrated as we could not find the hospital. So, we decided to return home, thinking it was way too far to walk. On the way back, we noticed a relatively large building with no windows. Our curiosity was aroused, and we decided to check it out.

When we went in, we discovered that the building belonged to Bank of America, with a branch on the ground floor and administrative offices on the upper floors. "Why not apply for a job in the bank?" we thought. The branch manager was Mr. Alex Bazerto. He was very gracious and courteous and gave us an application form. When we filled it out, Mr. Bazerto asked Leela to take a test. When she was about halfway through the test, he looked over what she had done and told her that was enough. And then he asked her: *"Can you start today?"* That was on Tuesday, September 24, 1974. We were not ready to start that day and asked permission to start the next day, and he consented. So, Leela began working for Bank of America on September 25, 1974, while carrying our firstborn for four months.

Once again, looking back, we can say with confidence and humility that the Lord ordered our steps, as the Word of God assures us. Psalm 37:23: *"The steps of a good man are ordered by the LORD: and he delighteth in his way."* (KJV). God's favor rested on Leela all the twenty-five years and eight months she served with Bank of America.

Since she was carrying, we decided that she would work only part-time until the baby was born. Since Fuller Seminary was very expensive, and I did not receive any financial aid, her part-time job alone was insufficient to meet all our obligations. So, I began to look around for odd jobs during weekends.

We had no car. Walking or taking a bus was our only option to get around. That made it challenging to look for odd jobs. Mike Mansperger, a classmate at Fuller, came to our rescue. He had an old VW beetle. Every Saturday morning, he would pick me up, and we would drive to a well-to-do neighborhood in Arcadia and do gardening work for a couple of families. For working all day, we would get paid $20 each. That was enough for a week's grocery for us.

Fuller had a notice board where people would post "help wanted" notices. One day late in 1974, I saw a message posted by Pasadena Foursquare Church. They sought someone to clean the church, teach a Sunday School class, and preach occasionally. In return, they were offering their old parsonage as housing. The offer was extremely attractive to us. So, we applied. The church was only about one and a half miles from Fuller Seminary. That was close enough to walk. Pastor Maurice Tolle,[43] was very kind and gracious to

---

[43] God used Pastor Maurice Tolle to lead Pastor Jack Hayford, a well-known pastor who founded Church on the Way, Van Nuys, California, to the Lord at age ten. Pastor Tolle served as a missionary in Latin America.

us and accepted our application. That was a great relief. No longer did we need to come up with the $110 a month as rent!

We moved to 182 Harkness Avenue, Pasadena, our home for the next five years, at the end of January 1975. The house was next door to Pasadena Foursquare Church, and it was the old parsonage. Since Pastor Maurice and Sister Hallie Tolle had their own house, the parsonage was vacant. Though it was old and rundown, for us, it was like a palace. It is the home where both our children were born.

Pastor and Mrs. Tolle were like parents to us. Later, when our children were born, they were like grandparents to them. Pastor Tolle dedicated both our children to the Lord. Finny and Renny were very fond of the Tolles. They loved to watch Pastor Tolle's blue Mercury Cougar coming in and going out of the church parking lot which was just behind our house!

In our hour of need, Pasadena Foursquare Church was the family that stood by us and helped us a great deal. We are ever grateful to Pastor and Mrs. Tolle and the congregation.

I started cleaning the church and helping Pastor Tolle in whatever way I could. I also started leading the youth group and teaching Sunday School. Pastor Tolle would occasionally ask me to preach for the Sunday evening service.

We had an active youth group. We got together regularly to play volleyball and badminton in the parking lot behind our house. It was a close-knit group. Even after all these years, some of us still stay in touch.

Leela took maternity leave starting on February 1, 1975. Dr. (Mrs.) Bower, the wife of a Professor at Fuller, was our gynecologist. Her office was very close to our new home. She was a very caring person and helped us a great deal. She asked us to take some classes together so that I could be with

Leela when the baby was born. We were excitedly looking forward to the birth of our first child.

As Leela's due date approached, we were very concerned. We had no car to get to the Sierra Madre Community Hospital, where the baby was to be born. Several friends were gracious enough to tell us to call them any time of the day or night and that they would help us to get to the hospital.

Leela started labor on the night of February 21. We called a friend from Fuller, Mr. Philip, who came quickly and took us to the hospital. The nurses who received us told Leela: *"Don't push. Dr. Bower is on the way. She will be here soon."*

They took us into the labor room and waited for Dr. Bower, who arrived very soon. Quickly, Leela was moved to the delivery room, and soon, our firstborn arrived, on the early morning of February 22, 1975- on the actual birthday of George Washington himself! What great joy it was to see the great gift that the Lord gave us! We named him Finny George Chavanikamannil after the great revival preacher Charles Finney, praying that the Lord would make him a great preacher like his namesake.

When Leela and the baby were discharged from the hospital two days later, our friend from the church, Lauren, came with his pickup truck to take us home. So, Finny's first journey was in Lauren's old pickup truck!

Our good friend from Fuller, Bob Fox, offered us his car when he realized we do not have a vehicle to take our baby to the doctor. He had won a Chevrolet Vega on the television show Price is Right. As he had another car, he did not need this one also. He told us that we could pay him little by little. He did not require a down payment, credit check, or any other stringent requirements that others would demand.

We could not have met any of these as we had no "credit" qualifications. It was so very gracious of Bob to do this to help us. And the price he charged us was just $1200. We were elated, agreed to his terms, took possession of the car, and paid him $200. We made regular payments to Bob until the vehicle was paid off.

Having a car helped me look for opportunities to earn a little more income as we now had a baby. Soon, I got a job to clean Immanuel Baptist Church in north Pasadena. That was a great help to us. That church family treated us very kindly. We didn't know the basics of caring for a baby, and there were no close family members to guide us and help us. Our church family helped us as much as they could.

We still remember vividly trying to give the first bath to the baby. As it was winter and relatively cold, we heated the room so hot to ensure that the baby didn't catch a cold from the bath! We both were afraid that we would drop him and hurt him. Giving a bath turned out to be a major production!

Leela was on maternity leave till March 31. When she returned to work, she opted for an evening shift in the administrative section of the bank, as we had no one to take care of our baby during the daytime when I had to attend classes at Fuller. So, she would take care of Finny till I returned after classes, and then she would go to work, and I would look after him. In between, we managed to clean two churches and, on Saturdays, worked as a gardener. Those were difficult days and, at the same time, very joyous days.

A few months after Finny was born, the Williams family moved into a house owned by Pasadena Foursquare Church. Mr. Keith Williams had retired from the Navy and was a student at Life Bible College. Mrs. Bonne Williams was fond of Finny and helped us to babysit him. They had four young children, and they all loved Finny

Chapter 7

A Miracle Through
the Los Angeles Yellow Pages

Mr. and Mrs. Wheat were members of our church. He managed a Kentucky Fried Chicken shop. Often, he would bring us KFC chicken because he knew we were struggling financially. One day, Mr. Wheat came to us with a copy of the Los Angeles Yellow Pages, which has two large volumes. I was not familiar with Yellow Pages at that time.

After giving the volumes, Mr. Wheat told us, "*I know you are struggling financially. George, you are a pretty good speaker. If you call some churches listed here, they might let you speak, which would help you.*"

I thanked him and took the books and kept them. I am a shy person. It is tough for me to ask anyone for any favors. So, I put the books away.

After a few weeks, as we struggled financially, I thought of following Mr. Wheat's advice. I picked up the Yellow Pages and opened it to the churches section. I could not believe my eyes! Pages after pages of churches. Hundreds and hundreds of listings. Which one am I going to call?

So, I did as in the old story of the man who wanted to find the will of God. He closed his eyes, opened the Bible, and pointed his finger to a verse. It read: "Judas hung himself." Not liking what he saw, he closed his eyes again, opened another page, and pointed his finger to a passage. Lo and behold, it read: "Go do likewise!"

I, too, prayed and opened the Yellow Pages and put my finger on a page. It read: "Berean Tabernacle." I dialed the number. A male voice answered: "West Los Angeles Christian Center. May I help you?" Though I was a bit confused by hearing a different name from what was printed in the Yellow Pages, I summoned enough courage to say something like: *"My name is George Chavanikamannil. I am from India, and I am a student at Fuller Theological Seminary. I would like to come and preach for you."*

There was silence at the other end for what appeared to me, in my nervousness, as an eternity. Then the person asked me: "When can you come?"

Since my calendar was completely free, I said: "How about next Sunday evening?" He said: "Come! We would love to have you."

I could not believe my ears. We had our first "invitation" to preach in a church other than our home church.

Next Sunday afternoon, Leela and I entrusted Finny with the Williams family and drove to Culver City, where the church was. Pastor Herb Maydwell and his wife Judy welcomed us warmly. They had recently become pastors of the congregation, which was known as Berean Tabernacle. They renamed it the West Los Angeles Christian Center. It was a small congregation of about sixty adults.

I spoke from the Word of God. People seemed to receive the message very warmly. The pastor was also pleased. He gave us a check for $50, a considerable amount for us in 1975.

As we said goodbye to all and were exiting the building, a young man at the door shook my hands. It was a "holy handshake"- he left something in my hand. It was a check for $25! The young man was Craig Reynolds, and that casual meeting was to impact our lives in ways neither of us could have imagined. He became a lifelong close friend. Craig eventually moved to India and married Jyoti, a godly Indian Christian lady. We will talk more about Craig and Jyoti as our story unfolds.

None of us could have foreseen what happened from what Mr. Wheat did when he counseled us to call churches for opportunities to speak and brought the Los Angeles Yellow Pages to us. Though I prayed before I opened the Yellow Pages and pointed my finger, I did not seriously think the Lord was directing my finger. Praise God for the sovereign grace of God, directing us moment by moment for His glory!

Pastor Herb kept inviting us back to preach and teach, and we became very close friends. He opened the door for us to Christian Evangelistic Assemblies (CEA), now known as Grace International, by introducing us to several key pastors in the fellowship. And CEA warmly embraced us and made us feel at home. That relationship, which began with the help of Mr. Wheat and the Los Angeles City Yellow Pages, blossomed into something very significant for the Kingdom of God, as will be seen as our story unfolds in the following pages.

Chapter 8

"God, Our Healer"

1977 and 1978 were very critical years for us as a family. As stated above, I have only one sister and one brother, both older than me. My sister, fourteen years older than me, has three sons and one daughter.

My brother was twelve years older than me. God blessed him with two daughters at first. In Indian culture, having a son is very important for most people. So, he started praying for a son, and the Lord blessed him with a son on August 31, 1972, the day Leela left for the US. According to our custom of naming children, he was named George, after his grandfather (my father). In our community, most children are given a "pet name" in addition to their "official name." Thus, he was given the "pet name" Biju.[44]

My brother enrolled Biju in LKG when he turned four at Saint Thomas Convent School, a Roman Catholic school run by nuns. Even at that tender age, Biju would pray for others. Nuns noticed that and often asked him to pray for them when any of them was not feeling well. And several nuns experienced healing when this little boy of four prayed for them.

One day, two of the nuns visited my brother and asked his permission to take Biju to pray for Cardinal Joseph Parecattil, a very prominent Cardinal of the Catholic Church

---

[44] It is ubiquitous among our people to have an "official name" and a "pet name." My parents gave all their children both. My sister's official name was "Achamma," after our paternal grandmother, and her "pet name" was "Leelamma." My brother's official name was "Oommen" after our paternal grandfather, and his "pet name" was "Joy"; my "pet name" is "Sunny."

in India, as he was suffering from severe pain in his hand. Biju laid hands on the Cardinal and prayed for his healing and he experienced instant relief from pain. The nuns were jubilant and joyously reported the news to my brother.

When God was using the little child in this manner, he began to fall ill frequently. At first it was very minor. Slowly the frequency and severity of the illness increased, By the time he was five, it became a bit serious to the point that the illness began to be of concern to the family.

Towards the end of 1977, when Biju was five years old, a family friend, who was well known in our circles as a devout prayer-warrior and a prophetess, prayed for my brother and family in a prayer meeting in my sister's home. Then she told my brother: *"Fast and pray so that the destroyer[45] will not enter your house."* My brother later confessed that he did not take that word very seriously.

Soon after that, small dark marks began to appear on his skin in different parts of his body. Slowly, some of those marks became sores. He would have high temperature fever. He was unable to eat anything as he had severe throat pain. He could not play or run around as he used to do. In the words of his older sister, Anila: *"Biju's countenance changed completely. He lost his child-like cute looks and appeared to be like an old man."*

On January 25th, 1978, his temperature became very high that he was rushed to the Kochi Port Trust Hospital.[46] Doctors there examined the child and ordered for blood work to be done and also prescribed some medications. It was

---

[45] Exodus 12:23 and Hebrews 11:28

[46] My brother's wife was an employee in the Kochi Port and, therefore, had access to this good hospital's services.

already evening and January 26th is India's Republic Day, a national holiday. So, blood test could not be done until 27th.

After returning home, my brother took Biju to family friends, Dr. Vincent Skaria and his wife Dr. Rosamma Skaria, both medical doctors, who had a clinic called Janatha Clinic nearby. Dr. Skaria did the blood work quickly. But, instead of telling anything to my brother, he put the result in a sealed envelope and gave it to him and instructed him to show it to the physicians in the Port Trust Hospital.

Later Dr. and Mrs. Skaria apologized to my brother and told him that they did not have the nerve to tell him the diagnosis because it was extremely serious. They were hoping that their test result was wrong and that the specialists' diagnosis in Port Trust Hospital would be different.

On the morning of January 27th, they took him again to the Port Trust Hospital and gave the physicians the test result from Janatha Clinic. They wanted to run their own tests. So, they ordered a slew of tests. Later in the day, when the results came, they called my brother privately and told him that Biju's illness was severe and he must consult Dr. Joy Chungath, a well-known pediatrician. Dr. Chungath was a pediatrician and consulting physician at the Port Trust Hospital. He also had a thriving private practice. He has many advanced degrees from very prestigious medical schools such as Christian Medical College, Vellore, and universities from USA and UK.

My brother went with Biju to consult him the next day morning. There was always a large crowd waiting to see him every day he opened his clinic. The day my brother went was not different. As he was holding Biju and leaning onto a mango tree outside the clinic, waiting for his turn, he heard this voice: *"Doctor will now tell you that Biju has leukemia. What will you do?"* It shook him thoroughly, and he wondered where the voice came from. He felt like crying aloud. At the same time, he did not want Biju to suspect anything. So, he composed himself.

Soon, his turn came to see Dr. Chungath. He examined the child and studied all the test results from the hospital and Janatha Clinic. Then he told my brother secretly, without Biju hearing as follows: *"Child has advanced leukemia. All his glands are swollen. With blood transfusion and available aggressive treatments, he might survive for a short period."*

You can imagine my brother's condition when he heard this news. My brother told Dr. Chungath that Biju had won first prize in a recitation competition at the school and that the child was eager to go to school and receive the award in front of everyone. The doctor's reply was: *"Why torture a child that has only a few days to live? Forget about sending him back to school."* My brother could not believe his ears.

Dr. Chungath ordered a few more tests to be conducted in Lisie Hospital, the best hospital in Kochi in those days. With that, my brother returned home, where everyone was waiting eagerly.

In those days, my parents and maternal grandmother lived with my brother. So, there were altogether eight members in the family. In addition, there was a family friend, Thanka, who helped with household chores ever since my brother's oldest daughter, Omana, was born. Thanka is virtually a family member and is still staying with the family.

Brother told the news only to the adults in the family. When Kochamma[47] heard the news, she vowed not to go to work and fast until the child is healed. She started wailing.

---

[47] What I called my brother's wife. This is a term of respect.

Hearing her cry, the two older children, Omana and Anila, understood that something was very seriously wrong. So, my brother had to tell them also. Biju's younger brother, Reji, was too young to understand what was happening. He was only a little over one year.

The whole family started crying and praying for the Lord's intervention. Both of Biju's older sisters were given an extraordinary measure of faith by the Lord and both tried to console the older adults and kept asking:

> *"Why are you crying? Are we not serving a living God? Is He not able to heal Biju?"*

Biju was too weak even to stand. So, they laid him down. He could not eat anything. Exhausted, he dosed off to sleep. When Kochamma laid down with Reji, Holy Spirit suddenly reminded her several Scriptures such as:

> *"Abraham believed God, and it was counted as righteousness to him."* (Romans 4:3). *"These signs shall follow them that believe. . ."* Mark 16:17. She also heard a voice: *"All of you lay hands on the child and pray. He will certainly be healed."*

Immediately she called everyone and asked them to surround the bed where Biju was sleeping, and lay hands on him and pray. My brother had gone outside to the nearby coconut grove to pray because he did not want others, especially Biju, to hear him crying. Omana and Anila went and called him. Everyone called on the Lord crying out to Him for mercy and grace. They kept praying for a long time.

Anila was eleven years old then. She had experienced the baptism of the Holy Spirit on December 5, 1976, little over a year and a month earlier. As everyone was praying, Holy Spirit came upon her with power. She laid her hand on Biju, and rebuked the evil one in the Name of Jesus. She spoke with authority and said three times in Malayalam as follows:

> *"You evil Satan, I command you to leave in the Name of Jesus."*

Then she sat down. Immediately everyone felt that something supernatural has happened. In an instant there was a change on Biju's face. He sat up and drank a cup of milk and then peacefully fell asleep.

Anila distinctly heard the Lord tell her three times the following:

> *"Tell your father these words: 'I have given Biju to you according to my promise. Why are you fearful? Fast and pray for seven days before me.'"*

Next morning, Biju got out of the bed and started playing! He asked for food and ate what Thanka gave him. His facial expressions and energy level had totally changed. He looked and acted like any other normal child of five. Everyone praised the Lord for the great miracle of healing. According to medical science he had only a few days to live. But here he was running around and playing.

Following the instructions given by Dr. Chungath, my brother took Biju to Lisie hospital on Saturday, January 28, 1978. They drew a lot of blood from different parts of Biju's body and ran all kinds of tests. My brother was still crying, hiding his tears from Biju. On the one side, there was the conviction that the Lord miraculously healed Biju the previous night. On the side, there was serious doubts.

> *Did it actually happen? Was Anila just saying all these because of her love for her brother? Did she really hear from the Lord?*

The hospital asked my brother to come back in the evening for the test results. When he went back, the nurse who assisted him in the morning came running to him with a big smile and told him that the child does not have the disease that the doctors suspected! All the tests have back negative! Biju is totally fine!

Once again, though he believed that the Lord had healed the child, my brother could not believe his ears. Is this real? He questioned the nurse and other people in Lisie hospital again and again. They all said that all the tests are negative. The child does not have leukemia!

My brother rushed to Dr. Chungath with the tests results. He carefully looked over all the test results. He was unable to believe what was right in front of his eyes. His words were: *"Are you sure that these are the results from Biju's blood?"* When my brother assured him that they were. Then he shared the story of what happened last night. After hearing my brother's testimony, Dr. Chungath said:

> *"I believe in God. Only God could have done this. This is a miracle. Medical science could not cure your son. God did. I am not prescribing any medications; just a few vitamins. Once the child gains strength, he can go to school."*

That Biju today, after more than four decades, is a professor in our Bible College in Dehradun. He continues to be in excellent health. Our God is a God who still heals the sick. By His death on the cross of Calvary, Jesus not only purchased forgiveness for our sins, but also healing and deliverance from our sicknesses. ". . . with his stripes we are healed!" (Isaiah 53:5b KJV).

Chapter 9

Family Grows and
World Vision Days Begin

On June 6, 1976, God blessed us with our second son, Renny. He was born in the Huntington Memorial Hospital in Pasadena on a Sunday evening. Coincidentally, June 6 is Martha Washington's birthday and also D-day. So, both our children were born on historically significant dates. *Is it just coincidence or the hand of God?*

The arrival of our second son brought us great joy. At first, Finny was very happy to see his brother. We have a few beautiful photographs showing his great pleasure in seeing his little brother. He was just over fifteen months old when his little brother arrived. Up to that point, he had been the center of attention. Then, all of a sudden, there was his younger brother, who was getting all the attention. That must have hurt him badly. So, one day, all of a sudden, we could not find him!

As our house was next to the church parking lot, we were always very concerned about his safety. We had made sure that the doors were shut so that he could not go out by himself into the parking lot as cars came in and went out fast.

Someone who came to see the new baby had left the back door open. Without anyone noticing, Finny got out and walked to the far end of the parking lot. When I came out running, frantically looking for the "missing" child, he was sitting on a rock there, totally dejected and sad! I can never forget the look on his sad face. He had convinced himself that no one wanted him because of the new baby, so he had decided to run away!

Leela would spend hours reading to the children. Since her shift in Bank of America was in the evening, she had ample time to teach the children during the day. She also helped them to memorize a lot of the Scripture. Because of her time with him, Finny had learned all the alphabet and how to count up to twenty before he was one! She still recounts how determined he was one evening to learn to count up to twenty before he went to sleep. Though exhausted, he refused to sleep until he ensured he had achieved his goal. We saw a remarkable determination in him even as a tiny baby.

He was reading fluently before he was two. When he was about two, a friend visited us from New York. She has children a little older than Finny and Renny. She could not believe Finny's reading skills. At first, she thought he had memorized the book's pages and was repeating from memory. So, she would ask him to read from random pages. He read with ease. And the books he was reading were not just picture books. These were books that older children could not read. Seeing his reading skills, she predicted that Finny would accomplish much in his life. We give all glory to God that her prediction has come true.

Renny also followed in his big brother's footsteps. We had to make several trips to the library every month. Even though we would check out the maximum number of books the library would permit, both would read all of the books so quickly that we had to go back within a day or two. We praise God that they became good readers and also memorized large portions of Scripture at their tender age. We believe that helped both develop their intellect and become good students.

Finny recited from memory the whole Christmas story as told by Luke (Luke 2:1-14) during the Christmas service in 1976 in Pasadena Foursquare Church when he was not even two. It became a regular habit for both children to memorize and recite large portions of the Scripture.

In 1976, a classmate at Fuller, Mike Marshall, approached me and offered me an opportunity to work for World Vision. Even in India, I had known World Vison to be a highly respected ministry. Moreover, Mike was a good friend. So, I said "yes" to Mike, who led World Vision's Telecommunication Center then.

The "Telecom Center," as it was commonly known, answered calls generated by the "telethons" that World Vision showed nationwide. "Telethons" were television shows that would run anywhere from one hour to five hours. These shows talked about the starving and suffering of humanity all across the globe. When a telethon was shown in a large television market like New York, we would receive tens of thousands of calls. We would have, at times, as many as 200 people answering the phones. It was an exciting place to work.

I started answering calls as a part-time employee. God gave me favor in the eyes of my superiors, and I very quickly received promotions and eventually became in charge of the center. In 1981, I was blessed to be chosen as the "employee of the year" from among the hundreds of people who worked for World Vision. Dr. Ted Engstrom, then President of World Vision, gave me a plaque with the following words engraved on it:

> *"1981 Award of Excellence presented to George Chavanikamannil in recognition of your character, achievements, and other qualities that exemplify Christian excellence at World Vision."*

All because of God's grace and mercy. God raised me up and blessed me beyond my wildest expectations. Dr. Engstrom became very fond of me and often encouraged me with his kind words. As will be seen later in the story, his friendship became a crucial factor in the founding and development of the Bible College/Seminary in India in just a few years.

I graduated from Fuller Theological Seminary on June 6, 1977, with a Master of Divinity (M.Div.) degree. God helped me to have an excellent GPA. So, I received admission for a Ph.D. in New Testament under the mentorship of Dr. Daniel Fuller. It was an unexpected privilege. But I regret to record that I never finished that degree as I got immersed in my work in World Vision. Failure to finish the Ph.D. from Fuller is a major regret in my life.

We continued to live in the Pasadena Foursquare Church parsonage till December 1979. God's favor was on Leela as she had also received several promotions in Bank of America. Our financial situation had significantly improved, so we were considering purchasing a house.

When we started looking to purchase a place, we found that Pasadena and the nearby places were extremely expensive and that we could not afford anything. So, we began to look in Azusa and Glendora, about 20 miles from where we lived.

Bank of America was very good to us and offered terms that we could afford. Because of that, we purchased our first home in the US at 1160 Morpath Lane in Glendora, California, and moved into that house in December 1979. Once again, we can only say, "Thank you, Lord, for your faithfulness." While millions born and brought up in the US are unable to purchase a home of their own, God, in His grace, allowed us, who came to the country with just $14 combined in our pocket and purse, to purchase a house for us in such a short time. How can we not thank Him and praise Him?

In the same month, I was blessed with the privilege of attending the famous Urbana Missions Conference on the campus of the University of Urbana, Illinois, organized by InterVarsity Student Fellowship. The first "Urbana" conference was held in 1946 in Toronto, Canada. Since then, tens of thousands of young people attend that conference every three years. Several prominent evangelical leaders such as Billy Graham, John Stott, and Mrs. Elizabeth Elliott preached in Urbana in 1979. It was a thrilling and challenging experience for me to sit under the powerful ministry of such great men and women of God. The conference added fuel to the burning desire that I already had to serve the Lord back in my home country.

We had enrolled Finny and Renny in Calvary Baptist Academy, a Christian school run by Calvary Baptist Church in Monrovia, California, as they both were very eager to go to school, though they were still too young for public schools to admit them. Calvary used a method known as Accelerated Christian Education (ACE) to teach the students. Every child was free to learn as much or as little as he or she desired. Children were not separated into classrooms according to their grades or ages. All were in one "learning center" supervised by "helpers" who helped them learn independently.

ACE system uses "paces" for each subject. A child can complete a "pace" in any given subject at her/his speed. Once a child completes the first "pace," s/he will go on to the second "pace," and so on. Both our children began to complete paces like no one had seen in Calvary Academy before. Finny and Renny finished off "paces" so fast that we could not afford to pay for them as each cost one dollar! Finny completed three grades in one year! By the age of six, he had completed all the requirements of grade five! Renny was right behind him. So, we had to make a decision. If they went at the pace they were going, they would complete all the requirements for high school before they were ten! And, to add to our dilemma, they both were physically small. Finny was so skinny that our friends at World Vision used to jokingly say: *"To get pictures of skinny children, we don't need to go to Africa; just take George's children's pictures!"*

After much prayer, we decided to take them out of Calvary Baptist Academy and enroll them in public school. By God's grace, Glendora had an excellent public school system. Willow School was within walking distance of our new home. So, we decided to put both the children there.

When we brought them to the school in 1981, the Principal told us they must attend classes according to their age. So, Finny had to go to class one because he was only six, and Renny went to UKG as he was five. We agreed. Two days later, we got a call from the Principal. When we went to the school, the teachers and Principal unanimously told us:

> *"It is very unfair to these children to ask them to remain in class one and UKG. They are way ahead of their peers. They would be bored and disinterested in their studies if we didn't challenge them. What should we do?"*

At the same time, looking at their physical development, all knew they would not fit in with the actual grades they should be studying, i.e., 5th and 3rd. So, we compromised and started Finny in class three and Renny in class one. They soon were helping their teachers as "teaching assistants" as they were ahead of all their classmates!

Finny & Renny

     Once we moved to our home in Glendora, I was released from the responsibility of cleaning Pasadena Foursquare Church, leading the youth group, and teaching Sunday School class. That allowed us to become fully involved in West Los Angeles Christian Center. So, we took up more responsibilities to help Pastor Herb. It was a long drive from Glendora to Culver City. But we loved the church family.

Looking back after all these years, we still say West LA Christian Center is the best congregation we were privileged to be a part of. Finny and Renny still talk about the potlucks in West LA church! Though a small church, it was full of caring and loving brothers and sisters in the Lord. We miss the warm fellowship of that little congregation.

Pastor Herb traveled with us to India in 1988 and witnessed our vision of starting a training center to train workers for the Lord's vineyard taking shape in Dehradun. He and Pastor Timothy Tennent even briefly joined the Bible College's construction team!

After Pastor Herb and Judy decided to move to Houston, Texas, Pastor Charles Paul and his wife Sylvia took charge of the congregation. Sadly, God called home both Pastor Charles and Pastor Herb and Judy. We look forward to being reunited with them in glory.

We made so many close friends in West LA Christian Center. Several of them are still very close to us, pray for us, and sacrificially help us with the ministries in India.

Moe and Lee Goulas became like grandparents to Finny and Renny. Whenever we needed help, they were there to help. Our children loved them. Since their own grandparents were in India and did not receive their love, Moe and Lee became very dear to them. They would come and stay with us whenever they could. We went on many trips together. We still miss them, even though they have been promoted to glory many years ago.

I enjoyed the ministry with World Vision and helping Pastor Herb preach and teach at the West LA Christian Center. Yet, the call to preach the Gospel in India was always in our minds. Leela and I kept praying and asking the Lord to lead us back to India in His time. We also told all our praying friends to pray with us for God's clear direction.

Chapter 10

Vision is Born

On the one hand, we longed to do what we could for the Lord in India. But, on the other side, there was a lot of fear and anxiety deep within us about returning to India as we knew how challenging any kind of Gospel ministry could be in that country. Therefore, we wanted to escape from the call. While serving the Lord with World Vision, I often wrestled with these conflicting emotions.

One day in 1984, sitting in my office at World Vision's Telecommunication Center, I took an adding machine. I did an arithmetic exercise to convince the Lord that it was useless for me to return to India! The population of India in 1984 was around 770 million. For the sake of convenience, I rounded it off to 800 million. Then, I theorized as follows. Suppose I return to India and preach to one thousand different people daily. If I can do it without taking even one day's break, how long will it take me to evangelize eight hundred million people?

I was shocked to realize that even if a person is actually able to do that,[48] it would take him or her 2,191.78 years to preach to 800 million people.[49] So, I told the Lord:

> *"Leave me alone. What's the use in forsaking our comfortable life in Southern California and going back to face all the difficulties in India? We will never be able to reach India with the Gospel."*

---

[48] I do acknowledge that it is humanly impossible to do this. It was only a theoretical formulation.

[49] Even if we took the actual population of India in 1984 as the base figure (766.8 million), it would take 2,100.82 years!

As soon as I thought that, the Holy Spirit very gently spoke to me:

"But what if there are 2,191.78 people doing that? It would take only one year!"

And immediately the Lord reminded me of His words in Matthew 9:37 and 38:

"The harvest truly is plenteous, but the labourers are few. Pray ye therefore the Lord of the harvest, that he will send forth labourers into his harvest." (KJV)

No one person or one organization can reach such a vast country with the Gospel. Crux of the problem that the Lord stated 2,000 years ago has not changed at all: a huge harvest field and very few laborers. *Multiplication of labourers is the key in reaching a place like India.*

As I was stunned by the realization of the "hugeness' of India, the Holy Spirit followed up with the challenge: *"Are you willing to do what you can?"*

There in my office in World Vision I made a covenant with the Lord:

"If you are calling me and commissioning me, I will go and do what I can to reach India with the Gospel."

It was then the Lord placed in my heart the vision to start a training center in North India to train and multiply laborers for the Lord's harvest.

The Indian subcontinent has other countries in it, not just India. There are Pakistan and Bangladesh with huge Muslim population, Nepal with its ardent Hindu and Buddhist people, and Bhutan that is virtually closed to the world. My heart breaks when I think of the millions still living without ever hearing the Gospel even once. I often feel so helpless when I think of these millions. At such moments of helplessness, the Holy Spirit reminds me again and again of the command of our Lord in Matthew 9. *He who knew the real condition of the world gave that command to us because that alone is the solution to the problem.* Let the Church rise up and cry out to the Lord of the harvest. Then we will see a breakthrough in reaching the millions who are still without witness. That conviction has only grown within me from that moment in 1984.

Donald McGavran's Influence

During my Fuller Seminary days, several great luminaries were teaching there. Preeminent among them were Dr. Donald McGavran, Dr. George Eldon Ladd, Dr. Daniel Fuller, Dr. Ralph Winter, Dr. Peter Wagner, and Dr. Geoffrey Bromiley, to name just a few. Dr. McGavran was a missionary to India for many years and knew India better than most Indians. Whenever he saw us, Indian students, on the campus, he would tell us:

> *"Go back to India and train your people; we Westerners are no longer allowed to become missionaries to India. Now it is your turn to equip the Church in India to fulfill the Great Commission of our Lord. Go and train your people."*

His counsel has echoed in my ears for years. When I had the encounter with the Holy Spirit, his words came back strongly in my memory. That strengthened the vision that God planted in my heart in the office of World Vision. From then on, we started asking the Lord to show us how to fulfill that nascent desire if it were His will.

At times we still had doubts in our hearts whether that was what God wanted us to do or whether that was an unrealistic "pipe dream." Yet, we kept praying and also sharing that dream with anyone who would listen to us.

Pastor Herb Maydwell and other pastors of CEA kept encouraging us in that dream. As we became more and more involved with CEA churches, many more doors opened for us to preach and teach in several churches. Pastor Orvel Taylor, pastoring the Colonial Tabernacle in Long Beach, invited us often to teach and preach for him. So did Pastors Paul Adams, Steve Riggle, William Carter, Billy Sanders Sr., and Jr., Mark Armstrong, and many others.

CEA, as a whole, embraced us with open arms and made us feel at home. I was ordained as a minister of the Gospel with Christian Evangelistic Assemblies on October 24, 1984, during the annual conference in Colonial Tabernacle, Long Beach, California. That was a very significant step in our ministerial development. We are ever grateful to CEA's leadership for welcoming us and making us part of that blessed ministry family.

Chapter 11

First Trip to India with Children

In December 1984, God opened the way for us to return to India as a family for the first time since Leela and I left India over a decade earlier. Our boys were excited to see their grandparents and to see India for the first time in their lives.

One day, we were doing some shopping before the trip. In 1984, there was a department store named Gemco in Glendora. We used to shop there regularly. When we reached the store, we saw that the employees were on strike, picketing the store, shouting slogans, and walking back and forth on the sidewalk in front of the store. Our boys had never seen anything like that before. When they asked us what was happening, we explained that the employees were on strike for better wages and benefits.

We flew Singapore Airlines to India. There was a break in our journey in Singapore. So, we decided to stay there for a few days and see Singapore. Singapore is one of the cleanest cities in the world. There is a substantial Indian population there. "Little India" is famous in Singapore with various Indian shops and restaurants.

We decided to have lunch in a restaurant called "Banana Leaf." It is a well-known Indian restaurant in "Little India." They serve meals on banana leaves, following an old South Indian custom. Our boys had never seen anything like that. When the banana leaves were spread before us, they thought those were placemats! But, when the waiter began to serve food on the banana leaf, they could not believe it. The boys tried to move away from us, and we heard Finny whispering to Renny: *Let's pretend that we don't know these people. They are primitive. They are eating from a leaf."* That was a huge culture shock for them. Many such surprises were

104

waiting for them in India. For Leela and me, it was reliving our childhood days when food for all festive occasions was served on banana leaves!

That night, on December 2, 1984, while in our hotel room, we heard the tragic news of the Bhopal gas accident. The news caught our attention primarily because my only sister's daughter, Daisy, and her husband- Rev. Mathews Varghese- were missionaries serving the Lord in Bhopal. We started praying for their protection and the protection of others in that thickly populated city. Unfortunately, thousands died from a chemical, methyl isocyanate (MIC), that leaked out of the Union Carbide's pesticide factory.

Lord miraculously protected our niece and her family. They were coming into the city on a train. Had they reached the city, they would have died because the railway station into which they were coming was very close to the point of the poisonous gas leak.

When the news of the gas leak reached the station master of the central railway station, he ran into his office, called all the outlying stations, and ordered them to stop all the incoming trains. *"Do not allow any trains to proceed into the city,"* he ordered. By that one action, he saved the lives of thousands of people. Later, he was found dead in his office, holding the phone in his hand. In his attempt to save others, he died. By one man's death, thousands were saved.

This brave man's story is an imperfect analogy of what the Lord Jesus did for all of us. By His death, the Lord Jesus made way for all to have eternal life. If by an imperfect man's death in Bhopal's central railway station, thousands could be saved, how much more by the death of the sinless, perfect Son of God? Thank you, Jesus, for dying for me and saving me from eternal death!

After our mini-vacation in Singapore, we flew to Madras (now known as Chennai). We landed at Madras airport around 11 at night. When we got out of the airport to catch a shuttle bus to Connemara Hotel, where we had booked a room as our flight to Kochi was only the next day, Renny, with a bewildered look on his face, asked us: *"How come everyone in Madras is on strike?"*

The streets were full of people. He had never seen anything like it before. The closest thing he has seen was the employees of Gemco on strike in Glendora! So, he thought that all the people in Madras must be on strike. Otherwise, why would all these people be on the street in the middle of the night? Another culture shock for our children!

The next day, we reached Kerala. Seeing both sets of our dear parents and siblings after so many years was a special joy. All were eagerly waiting to see us, particularly Finny and Renny. For the next several weeks, we visited scores of relatives and friends.

For our children, almost everything was completely new and different- from drawing water from a well for a shower *("How many cups of water should I put on my head,"* was a question Finny asked as he took his first "shower"!!!), to seeing the overcrowded buses, stalks of bananas in different sizes and colors hanging in front of every village shop, seeing people plowing fields with oxen, bullock carts loaded to the hilt with all kinds of strange-looking things, just to name a few.

Most educated people in India speak English (India is supposedly the largest English-speaking country in the world!). But Finny and Renny's accent was challenging to follow, even for their cousins, who all spoke English well. So, they would ask them to slow down or, at times, if they could not still understand them, say: *"Spelling, please!"*

Walking through the village roads where I played as a child and seeing my buddies with whom I grew up was a great joy. It brought back vivid memories of my joyous childhood. Many of my friends had gone abroad for jobs, most to the United Arab Emirates, Kuwait, Bahrain, and Saudi Arabia. I missed seeing them. Seeing their elderly parents and reminiscing about the bygone days was particularly joyous.

We greatly missed my maternal grandmother. She had gone to be with the Lord on July 12, 1982, two and a half years earlier. That put a damper on our visit. My parents kept reminding us how she wanted to see Finny and Renny. We have to wait till glory for her to see them.

A significant event during our visit was the wedding of Leela's younger sister, Valsamma. Wedding customs in our culture are unique in so many ways. Many of the customs that we find in the Bible pages are still part of Indian weddings. Sadly, that is changing slowly as Western influence is affecting these customs, especially the traditions and practices of Christians.

We also traveled to North India. I had never been to North India before. Leela has been to North as she was a teacher in Kathmandu, Nepal before she moved to the USA.

Valsamma's husband, Johnson, was an officer in the central secretariat of the Government of India. We stayed with them in their apartment in New Delhi and they helped us to tour Delhi and Agra. We visited several important historical sites in Delhi such as Mahatma Gandhi's residence and the place where he was assassinated, Mrs. Indira Gandhi's residence and the spot where she was assassinated, and the famous Red Fort, etc.,

In Agra, we toured the magnificent Taj Mahal, one of the seven wonders of the world. It is a mausoleum built by the Mughal Emperor, Shah Jahan, as a memorial to his beloved wife Mumtaz Mahal. Queen Mumtaz passed away from postpartum hemorrhage while she gave birth to her 14th child. It took almost twenty years to build with twenty thousand people working every day!

As one of the Government of India's tourism promotion slogans says: *"Today men get away with a bunch of roses (to show their love)!"*

Then we went to the holy city of Banaras (Varanasi) on the banks of the Ganges river, where Leela's cousin, Rev. K. V. Abraham (Babychayan), who took her to Nepal in 1964, was leading the ministries of New Life League. We stayed with him, and he took us around the city. Our hearts were once again broken by seeing the multitudes crowding on the banks of the Ganges seeking salvation. Many dead bodies were being cremated on the banks of the river as it is considered auspicious by many.

We also spent time with my nephew, George C. Kuruvilla, Rev. K.J. Kuriakose, T.S. Sam, and others who were then serving the Lord with Rev. K.V. Abraham.

We have constantly asked the Lord for His specific direction in our lives. We knew the Lord wanted us to serve Him in North India. Yet, we did not know where in North India. Part of our decision to visit the North was with the hope that the Lord would speak to us clearly and direct our steps. So, as we traveled, we kept praying:

"Lord, lead us to the <u>exact place</u> you want us to be in North India."

One day, during our travels, God told us it was time to take up our call to North India. Still, He did not tell us where to go- only that it was time to move.

Chapter 12

Stepping Out in Faith:
Resignation from World Vision

When we returned to the US in January 1985, I submitted my resignation to my boss, Mr. Marty Lonsdale. He already knew our desire to return to India to do something for the Kingdom in India. And he was glad for that commitment. Yet, he told me that I could not leave right away and that I must give him a little more time to find and train a replacement for me. So, we mutually agreed that January 15, 1986, would be my last day with World Vision.

There was great peace in our hearts about our decision, even though we had no idea what our next steps were. There were many unanswered questions in our minds: *where exactly in India were we to go to, what precisely were we to do, where would the needed resources come from?*

Despite all the uncertainties, there was peace in our hearts. Many people told us that what we were planning to do was foolish. They were well-meaning people but did not understand God's call. They told us words like these:

> *"You are already touching the world through World Vision. Why do you want to leave that and go to India? Don't you know that North India is very hostile to the Gospel? What would happen to the future of your children?"*

When you have the call of God on you, nothing other than obeying that call will satisfy you. Only those who have received a call can understand what Jeremiah describes in 20:9:

"If I say, 'I will not mention him, or speak anymore in his name,' there is in my heart as it were a burning fire shut up in my bones, and I am weary with holding it in, and I cannot."

The evil one also put great fear in our hearts. The greatest fear was concerning the future of our children. God has blessed us with two sons, and both are very brilliant. In the Indian culture, as in most cultures, education is highly valued. One question that came up often in our mind was how we would provide good education to our children if we followed our call.

We parents are willing to suffer poverty and hunger but cannot even bear the thought of our children suffering. We have seen Satan using the fear of children's future to prevent several people from pursuing their God-given calls. We, too, almost fell prey to that.

As the end of a paycheck for me was fast approaching, this fear began to increase rapidly. In October 1985, when I had only two more months left with World Vision, I attended the CEA annual conference in Roseburg, Oregon. I went to the meeting, desperate to hear from God. I was crying out to the Lord in my spirit to make it clear whether He was really calling us or whether all this was my sheer imagination.

During one evening meeting, the Holy Spirit moved very powerfully. When the preacher gave the altar call, I was one of the first to run to the altar. I was desperate to hear from the Lord. I went to a corner of the altar, knelt there, and cried to the Lord, asking Him to speak to me and lift the heavy fear I was experiencing. I was careful to hide my tears. A few moments later, someone came near me, laid hands on my shoulders, leaned over to my ears, and softly said: *"Jehovah Jireh!"*[50]

It was a woman's voice. Though she spoke very softly, it was like a peal of thunder in my soul! *The moment those words entered my ears, I felt a sovereign peace coming over me and all the fears vanishing.*

Yet, the very next instant, the enemy succeeded in sowing seeds of doubt within me. Instantly the thought came: *"Oh, it must be someone who knows your situation and just said those words to console you."* So, I wanted to see who the person was that spoke to me. I opened my eyes and looked. She was a total stranger to me.

At the end of the altar service, I went looking for that lady. I wanted to make sure. I found her and introduced myself to her and learned that her name was Carol Allen, and she was from Fort Wayne, Indiana. Pastor Ron Allen, her husband, and Carol were pastors of a Vineyard Church and had come to attend the conference. She did not know me at all.

I asked her: *"Why did you tell me Jehovah Jireh?"*

She was taken back a little with my question and asked me: *"Did I say or do anything wrong?"* I told her "No" and explained why I was questioning her. I just wanted to make sure that it was the Word of the Lord. Carol did not know anything about me and felt strongly that the Lord had given her that Word for me. Then I told her that the very

---

[50] Genesis 22:14. In Hebrew, "Yahweh Yireh," the name Abraham called the mountain on which he sacrificed his one and only son, Isaac. The phrase means, "The Lord will provide," referring to the miraculous way in which God provided a ram for Abraham to sacrifice and spared the life of Isaac.

111

instant she uttered those words, I knew that the Lord spoke to me, and my fears evaporated from my spirit.

I returned from that convention with a renewed conviction that it was the Lord who was directing us to leave World Vision and that He would provide for all our needs. Yet, I must confess that I had no inkling in my mind of how He would so gloriously fulfill that promise! I kind of limited that promise to the ministry's needs in my narrow-mindedness and did not at all apply it to our children's future. How gracious our Lord is! Despite our lack of faith, He, in His faithfulness, miraculously provided for our children. Even in our wildest imaginations, we could not have conjured up the beautiful ways in which the Lord would bless our children.

The Lord provided miraculously for the education of both of our boys. Finny, our older son, received full scholarship from Harvard University, arguably the best University in the US to do double doctorate degrees: MD in Medicine and Ph.D. in Chemistry. Along with these two doctoral degrees, he also did a Master's in Computer Science and Electrical Engineering from Massachusetts Institute of Technology (MIT), all paid by the National Science Foundation! God also made it possible for our younger son to graduate from the University of California, Irvine (UCI).

Both our children have been immensely blessed by the Lord, far more than we could even dream of. More than anything else, both, along with their families, love the Lord and are serving the Lord.

Now, looking back, we can say with confidence that the Psalmist is one hundred percent accurate when he wrote: *"Those who look to him are radiant; their faces are **never** covered with shame" (Psalm 34:5).* Our God is a God who keeps His promises and rewards those who trust Him.

We continued to pray, seeking God's face. As we did not know where we were supposed to go in North India, we continued to specifically pray one sentence: *"Lord, lead us to the exact place you want us to be in North India."*

Though we used the words, *exact place*, what we meant was the city/town/state where God wanted us to locate the ministry. Frankly, we did not expect the Lord to answer our prayer precisely. Yet, He did answer and miraculously led us to the exact spot He had chosen for us. (Chapters 13 and 14 describe in detail how the Lord did it). His ways are indeed far higher than ours!

On January 15, 1986, I bid "goodbye" to my colleagues at World Vision Telecommunication Center, which was "home" to me for almost ten years. It was a bitter-sweet goodbye as I loved working with World Vision. At the same time, I knew that the Lord was calling us for the purpose for which He created us- to give our lives for His Church in North India.

Chapter 13

God Directs Us to Dehradun

I was off to India the following day. Except for the short visit in early 1985, I had never traveled in North India. I am not fluent in Hindi, the dominant language of North India.[51]

So, I asked my sister's son, a missionary in North India, to travel with me. We call him Babu. His official name is George C. Kuruvilla. As he is my sister's second son, he was given my father's first name according to our custom of naming children. His father's first name was Kuruvilla, and "C" is the short form for his family name- Chempakaserril.

Babu came to Banaras (ancient name: Varanasi)[52] on July 13, 1976, right out of high school at nineteen with his childhood friend, K.J. Kuriakose. They studied at the New Life Bible College (NLBC) in Varanasi. The director of NLBC was Leela's first cousin, Rev. K.V. Abraham, who took Leela to Nepal, as stated above.

After he graduated from NLBC, he started serving the Lord with the New Life League under the leadership of Rev. K.V. Abraham. He became very seriously ill and almost lost his life in 1979. God, in His mercy, spared his life and allowed him to faithfully continue his service to the Kingdom in Banaras and the surrounding areas. In many places in

---

[51] Hindi is India's national language, while English is India's official language. India has close to five hundred living languages. In our school days, we were taught that there are 1,652 languages in India. Many of these have now died down. The estimated number of living languages varies between 450 and 500, depending on whose survey one trusts.

[52] Varanasi in one of oldest living cities in the world along with cities such as Jerusalem, and Baghdad.

Eastern Uttar Pradesh, he and his colleagues were attacked and chased out for preaching the Gospel. By God's grace, there are vibrant worshipping congregations in all those places today.

As he is very fluent in Hindi and thoroughly knows the North Indian culture, he became a great help to me. He and his wife, Laly (whom we fondly call Lalamma), became our righthand people in building up the ministry. Leela and I are ever grateful to both of them for their faithfulness and hard work for the Lord.

We traveled through several states of North India. Wherever we went, we would meet with local Christian leaders who would give us appointments. We shared with them our vision to build a small training center to train church planters. We took care to emphasize the word *"small"* as we had no resources at our disposal. We had only a dream and the conviction that the Lord had called us and given us the vision to train a few men and women to reach the unreached in the Indian subcontinent.

During our travels, we visited the city of Gorakhpur in the state of Uttar Pradesh. We had heard that Operation Mobilization (OM India) was having its national leadership camp there. So, we decided to go there, hoping to get an opportunity to meet OM India leaders and seek their counsel. OM has had a tremendous impact on the evangelization of India. OM leaders graciously welcomed us. We attended a couple of meetings and met with several leaders.

One of the leaders who met with us was Brother Ray Eicher, one of two All India Coordinators of OM India (the other being Alfred Franks). After hearing our vision, he told us to visit the city of Dehradun before we finalized our plans. He told us that the world-famous Woodstock School, founded by missionaries to teach their children, was in Mussoorie, just thirty kilometers from Dehradun. We could enroll our children there for their schooling and start the training center in Dehradun, a hill station with moderate weather compared to North India's plains.

At that time, we had no intention of going to Dehradun as we knew Doon Bible College (DBC), one of the oldest Bible Colleges in North India, was there. We thought that we must go to a place where there was no Gospel witness rather than a place where there was already a Bible College. When we shared that thought with Brother Ray, he counseled us to look at Dehradun before finalizing our plans.

Respecting his counsel, Babu and I reached Dehradun on the evening of January 31, 1986. The Principal of DBC then was Brother Jacob Chacko (now Dr. Jacob Chacko), who had taught Babu at New Life Bible College, Banaras. Since Babu knew him, we went directly to meet Brother Jacob. He and his wife, Susie, warmly welcomed us, gave us dinner, and hosted us in the DBC guest room.

Upon hearing our plans, Brother Jacob enthusiastically encouraged us to choose Dehradun. When we expressed our reservations about starting another training center in the city where there were two Bible Colleges/Seminaries,[53] he assured us that there was a great need for more training centers in North India and that Dehradun was an ideal location. He informed us that DBC was maxed out in its capacity to admit trainees. They were getting far more applicants than they could accept as they had no space in their dormitories.

When we met with Pastor T.J. Simon, then pastor of Masih Mandli, one of the first Pentecostal congregations in

---

[53] After reaching Dehradun, we learned that the Presbyterial Theological Seminary (PTS) was also there. When we met with the leadership of PTS, to our surprise, they, too, were positive about our coming to Dehradun!

North India, he too ardently asked us to come to Dehradun. So too, all the faculty members of DBC. Brother Narendra Katare, the Registrar of DBC, especially encouraged us to locate the training center in Dehradun. Only one person discouraged us from establishing the school in the city, and that person was a Western missionary, a visiting teacher at DBC. Later, as we met and talked to a few faculty members of the Presbyterian Theological Seminary (PTS), they, too, welcomed us. We did not at all expect such a warm welcome from either of these institutions. We began to feel that the counsel of Brother Ray Eicher was from God.

Brother Jacob Chacko drove us around Dehradun and introduced us to several influential Christian and non-Christian leaders. I liked the location when I saw the majestic foothills of the Himalayas that virtually surrounded the city and the land layout. I felt drawn to the place. I had no idea of the region's spiritual significance at that time.

We kept fervently praying the one prayer every day:

"Lord, lead us to the exact place that you want us to be in North India."

After some initial calculations, we decided to acquire at least five acres of land for the planned training center. Now, five acres in my mind was vast. I grew up on a farm in Kerala that was hardly three acres. That was a big place in my mind. So, I thought that if we had five acres, we could build all the needed buildings in that space.

One of the people that Principal Jacob Chacko introduced us to was a businessman, Mr. Swain. He was a real estate agent.[54] Mr. Swain told us that getting five acres near the downtown area is impossible. But if we were willing

---

[54] The common term in India is "broker".

to go a little outside of the city, he would be glad to help us to get the land. Mr. Swain also informed us that we could expect to pay at least one hundred thousand Rupees for an acre.[55] He told us to come with five hundred thousand Rupees and that he would get us five acres. We asked him to look for land and promised that we would return with the funds soon.

Babu and I turned our attention to registering a Society[56] as the next step in pursuing our vision. We sought the help of several Christian leaders to become members of the Society, and God gave us favor with them. Rev. C. George, my cousin who asked me in 1972 to serve the Lord with him in Every Home Crusade, was stationed in New Delhi as the Asian Director of Christ Groups, the church-planting ministry of World Literature Crusade. He graciously consented to serve as the Chairman of our Board. Because of his name and influence several others consented to help us.

After entrusting Babu to follow up with that process, I returned to the US in April 1986 just in time to file our taxes.

---

[55] At that time one US dollar was approximately equal to ten Indian Rupees. So, one acre of land outside of the city would cost about $10,000.

[56] As India was a British colony for over 200 years, we still use many British terms. Society is a 501 (c) 3 Corporation in the US.

Chapter 14

Jehovah Jireh **Proves Himself!**

Leela and I planned to move our whole family to India within a year or so. I visited Woodstock School in Mussoorie and picked up application forms to enroll Finny and Renny in the boarding school. We thought we would live in Dehradun, and the children would study in Woodstock, residing in the boarding school.

Two factors changed our plans. Looking back now, we know that it was the Lord who, once again, sovereignly directed our steps. How gracious is our God, who, in His wisdom, leads us by our hands!

When we announced the boarding school plans, Renny, our younger son, reacted almost violently. He was only nine then. We still remember practically verbatim what he said to us. After saying that he does not want to go to a boarding school, with tears, he said:

> *"When I grow up, I will become the Prime Minister of India and ban all boarding schools!"*

He made it very clear that he did not want to go to a boarding school. What do we do now?

God speaks through Paul Van Oss:

I shared the incident with a friend from World Vision, Paul Van Oss. Paul was a wise man with a lot of experience in different ministries. His wife, Barbara, was my colleague in the Telecommunication Center, and they both prayed for us faithfully. Paul counseled us as follows:

> *"You must keep a foot in the US to see the ministry develop in India. Without adequate funding, a seminary cannot grow and function, and the Church*

in North India is not strong enough to support the development of a seminary."

His words made sense. Leela and I started to pray, considering our younger son's adamant refusal to accept a boarding school and Paul's wise words.

After waiting on the Lord in prayer, we decided that Leela would continue to work for Bank of America and take care of the children and that I would commute to India until such a time when the children would be old enough to be on their own. We knew full well that it would be challenging for both of us, particularly for Leela. Yet, God gave us the grace to press on with that altered plan.

High School Graduation Photos of Finny and Renny

Looking back over almost four decades, we can affirm fully that Paul Van Oss's counsel was from the Lord. God blessed that decision we took. He blessed the ministry by providing all the needed resources. He also blessed both our children far more than we ever dreamed possible.

However, it was not an easy decision. Neither was it easy to execute. Being apart for extended periods was extremely hard for both of us. Leela's task was the hardest. Holding down a very responsible job with Bank of America and caring for two minor children was extremely challenging for her. There were no family members to help us out. She had to carry the burden by herself. I will ever be grateful to her for the sacrifices she made. All we have accomplished in India is primarily due to her willingness to carry a heavy burden without even one word of murmuring or complaint. I have seen several men with far more extraordinary talents and giftings than me failing to accomplish much in life because their spouses were either unwilling or incapable of making sacrifices. I continually praise God for my beloved. She is indeed the best that has happened to me, second only to the Lord Jesus.

1986 is a critical year in our story. As stated above, January 15, 1986, was my last day with World Vision. God promised us that He is *"Jehovah Jireh"* in October 1985 during the CEA annual convention in Garden Valley Church, Roseburg, Oregon. We began to see the fulfillment of that promise as soon as we stepped out in faith by resigning from my job.

When I left World Vision, we had no idea how we would fulfill our vision of training leaders for the Church in North India. We hardly had any resources. A few of our close friends had promised us one thousand dollars a month by way of personal support. It does not take a rocket scientist to determine that one cannot establish a training center with such limited resources.

But, once we took the step of faith, we began to see God move. We see this fundamental spiritual principle all through the Scripture. Only when the children of Israel stepped into Jordan did the river part.[57] It was only after the multitude sat down on the green grass in groups by hundreds and by fifties that Jesus multiplied the five loaves and two fish.[58] Only when, in obedience to His command, people removed the stone that had closed the tomb did Jesus raise Lazarus from the dead.[59] We must first take the step of faith and obey. *When we do what we can in obedience to the Lord's command, He will do what we cannot and reveal His glory. Faith is obedience.* We began to experience this in 1986 *after* we stepped out in faith, not *before*. We do walk by faith and not by sight.[60]

As mentioned, I returned from India in April 1986, just in time to file our income tax returns. Soon after, we organized *Good News for India* as a subsidiary ministry of *Christian Evangelistic Assemblies* to raise funds to build the training center. Pastor Herb Maydwell consented to be the Chairman, and several of our friends from West Los Angeles Christian Center and World Vision agreed to serve as Board Members.

We started knocking on doors to raise the five hundred thousand Rupees (roughly fifty thousand dollars) needed for the five acres of land in Dehradun. We put it as a "fleece" before the Lord, just like Gideon did in asking to confirm his call.[61] Though we were sure of our call, we wanted to make it doubly sure. Therefore, we asked the Lord

---

[57] Joshua 3:15.

[58] Mark 6: 39-42.

[59] John 11:39-44.

[60] 2 Corinthians 5:7.

[61] Judges 6.

to provide the funds only if it were His perfect will for us to go forward with our plans.

June and July 1986 proved to be critical months for us. Three important events that have far-reaching effects on our vision happened during these months.

God speaks to the leaders of World Vision:

First was a call from Marty Lonsdale, my boss and good friend from World Vision. He asked me to meet him in his office in Monrovia, California. When I met Marty, he told me that World Vision has decided to help us.

I thought that they might write a big check! Instead, Marty told me to meet Randy Miller, the editor of World Vision magazine.

I knew Randy well. Soon, Randy was interviewing me for an article in the next issue of the magazine. I never expected such great help.

World Vision magazine went to over a million households!

***The first unexpected event in God fulfilling His promise
that He is "Jehovah Jireh"- World Vision published the
above article about us in the August-September 1986 issue.***

As Randy and I discussed the vision the Lord had
given us, he abruptly asked me: *"George, how much money
would it take for you to build this school?"*

I had not at all thought about that. I was trying to raise
fifty thousand dollars to buy land. Now he is asking me about
the cost of the whole project. What do I do? How can I tell
him I do not know? What would he think of me if I did not
reply quickly? All these questions were swirling around my
head in a nano-second. I breathed a prayer saying: *"Lord help
me!"* Then I blurted out: *"Two hundred thousand dollars."*

As I walked out of Randy's office, I was kicking myself. *"Why Did I say that amount? On the one side, that's a lot of money. On the other hand, to build an institution that is not enough."* All these thoughts pummeled me. I tried to forget the interview. But to no avail. I had no idea that the Lord put that amount in my mouth. Months later, I learned that God had prepared a widow in Elberton, Georgia, who had no idea I even existed, to help us. She had precisely that amount in her mind and was looking for a sign from the Lord to identify a ministry to help! *God, who prepared a widow in Zarephath to help Elijah, is still living, and He was working behind the scenes to help us even though we did not have the faith to trust Him.*

The article came out in the 1986 August-September issue of World Vision magazine. I expected only a paragraph or two in a corner of a page. I was surprised to see the article covered two full pages. Randy included my picture, too! More than that, he gave Good News for India's mailing address at the end with the caption: "Write to George Chavanikamannil for further information about Good News for India."

It was a very well-written article. And it began to generate letters from all over the world! We got letters from Africa, Korea, Canada, and, of course, from many states in the US. Many letters had checks in them!

I was "on the road," almost continually trying to communicate our vision to anyone who would listen. Jim and Beverly Jones, good friends from West Los Angeles Christian Center, had volunteered to receive letters, deposit checks, and send receipts. Jim would give me letters that he thought I should see. He took care of all the rest.

In the meantime, World Vision gave me an office to use as and when I needed it. In 1986, laptops were not available. We could not afford an office computer. So, World

Vision's help was invaluable as the office had a desktop and a printer that I could use.

One day, Jim came to me with a few letters. Two of them turned out to be extremely important. One letter with an enclosed check was from a young Methodist pastor, Rev. Timothy Tennent, and his wife, Julie, from Nacoochee, Georgia. He informed us that they are very interested in India and would like to meet and discuss our plans to train Indian Christians to preach the Gospel and plant churches. We started corresponding with each other. As a result, Tim and Julie became life-long friends who have contributed immensely to the founding, growth, and development of the Bible College/Seminary and related ministries in India.

Coincidentally, the second letter was also from Georgia! When Jim handed that letter to me, he said:

"George, I almost threw this letter out. Look at the handwriting. It looks like that of a child to me. But I didn't want to throw it out without showing it to you."

A careful look at the letter dispels such thoughts both by the penmanship and content of the letter. The letter dated August 24, 1986, stated:

"Dear Sir:

I read in a magazine that you are desirous of establishing an Evangelism College in North India to train Indians in evangelization. I also read in our State Baptist paper, "Christian Index," that foreign funds are denied for Indian missionaries. We have some Southern Baptist Missionaries. If foreign funds are not approved, the Mission could be forced to sell vehicles and land plots or buildings. Would this affect your project?

How much money you would need to get your project underway? Of course, you would want to build for the future and erect buildings that could be continued to be used in the years ahead. Please let me hear from you.

Sincerely

Janie New

I read the letter on September 4, 1986, sitting in the office that World Vision had given me for my use. As I read the letter, I felt that I heard these words:

"Something very significant will happen with this person."

Those words were so clear that I turned around to see who spoke. Of course, there was no one there. I realized that it was the Holy Spirit who spoke those words. So, I immediately wrote a reply. As I started to write, the same voice that I heard earlier spoke again and told me:

"She made clear that she is a Southern Baptist. Make sure you let her know who you are."

So, I opened the letter by stating that I am an ordained Pentecostal preacher with Christian Evangelistic Assemblies. As CEA is a relatively small fellowship, Mrs. New may never have heard of us. So, I put in parenthesis "like Assemblies of God," assuming she must have heard of AG. Then, I shared my testimony and the vision to train servants of God for the Church in India. I sent off the letter and waited for her reply.

We received no reply from her in September or October. Once in a while, I remembered the voice I heard, which I thought was of the Holy Spirit. Then I would think that all that was just my imagination and tried to forget Mrs. New and her letter.

By the end of September, God had helped us raise the target amount to purchase the land. After consulting with the Board, I decided to go to India to acquire the land. Before leaving for India, I wanted to attend the annual CEA convention scheduled for the last week of October 1986.

We will come back to this point a little later. Before that, let me share two other significant events in June/July 1986.

God speaks through Leela.

We invited Pastor Herb and Judy, Jim and his wife Beverly, and a few other close friends for dinner. Leela cooked delicious chicken curry and several other Indian dishes. After dinner, we were sitting around talking. All of a sudden, Leela spoke up and said:

> *"We are trying to raise fifty thousand dollars to buy five acres of land in India. Once we buy the land, what will we do with it?"*

After pausing for several moments, and as no one said anything, she continued:

> *" If we ask the Lord, He will give us the land for half the price. Then, we will have some money left to build something in the property."*

As soon as she finished speaking, Pastor Herb spoke up and said:

> *"That's the Lord's counsel to us. Let's pray."*

We all held our hands around the dining table, and Pastor Herb prayed, asking the Lord to give us five acres of land in India for twenty-five thousand dollars. The following Sunday morning, he announced it from the pulpit and invited the whole church to pray. Jim, our accountant friend, printed a sizeable dot-matrix banner and hung it in the foyer of the

West Los Angeles Christian Center that read: *"Five acres for twenty-five thousand dollars in India!"*

I thought that all of this was rather presumptuous. We had talked to several real estate agents (the term in India is "brokers") in Dehradun. All of them had quoted a minimum of a hundred thousand Rupees for an acre. Now we are praying for fifty thousand Rupees for an acre! I did not feel that it was from the Lord. But I kept my mouth shut. I did not even attempt to go to India to purchase the land until we had raised five hundred thousand Rupees, proving that I did not believe in this prayer that my wife and our Pastor had initiated.

Though I did not believe or pray, God, in His mercy, honored the prayers of Pastor Herb, my wife, and the other saints of West Los Angeles Christian Center, as will be seen later in the story. Here is another important spiritual principle: *God works for His glory even when we do not trust Him as we ought to trust Him. It is often not because of our faith that the Lord works. It is despite our lack of faith!*

God's Grace and Miraculous Deliverance:

We must share a miraculous experience as the Lord prepared to show us His glory. One night early in June 1986, I had a nightmare. In the dream (nightmare), we, as a family, were visiting a friend who had a pool in his backyard. Children were all playing in the pool while adults sat around and talked.

Suddenly, I looked up and found Leela standing on the pool's diving board. Instantly, I knew the pool was not deep enough for her to dive. But before I could run out and stop her, she dived into the pool. She was not coming back up! So I jumped into the pool and lifted her up. She was dead! She had a cut across the forehead. She was dry, not wet

129

at all, though I had just picked her up from the bottom of the pool!

By then, I woke up from the nightmare terrified. I checked on Leela. She was fast asleep next to me. I checked and made sure she was breathing! Then, I prayed for a while and fell back asleep. Morning came. I completely forgot the dream/nightmare.

Leela needed to drive to Pasadena for her work at Bank of America. She did not have enough petrol in the car, and she hated filling the vehicle. So I drove with her to the nearest gas station, filled her car, and sent her off to work. I heard the phone ringing when I returned home and opened the garage. The dream returned to my memory as soon as I heard the phone. A California Highway Patrol (CHP) officer was at the other end when I answered the phone. He very calmly told me: *"Your wife is in an accident. Come."* Then he gave me the location.

I was terror-stricken, having the nightmare the previous night. As I rushed to the scene of the accident, fire engines, ambulances, and police vehicles were already there. To my great relief, I saw Leela standing and talking to police officers. *When I got near her, she had the exact same cut on her forehead that I saw in my nightmare!* But she was fine. There was not another scratch on her body, though the car was totaled. The CHP officer told me that we were lucky that Leela was not decapitated! She had lost control of the vehicle and it went under the heavy wire that separates the freeway from oncoming opposite traffic. The top of the car, starting with the bottom of the windshield, was sliced off like someone cutting paper with scissors! How the wire missed her neck/head was a miracle, according to the CHP officer!

The Lord had warned me the night before in that dream/nightmare. He gave me the grace to pray for a long time. I am convinced that the evil one was attempting to thwart our call by taking Leela's life. God's immeasurable grace protected her life and delivered us from the evil one's schemes. All glory to God alone!

God speaks through an architect's model:

Pastor Steve and Becky Riggle have been good friends since we met them through Pastor Herb and Judy Maydwell. They had pioneered a congregation in Livermore, California. In 1983, God called them to Houston to plant a church there. They invited me to speak at Grace Community Church, the congregation that they were pioneering. I was with them during the weekend of June 21-22, 1986.

Then Grace Community Church met for worship in League City, just outside of Houston. Pastor Steve asked about our plans, and I informed him that we were trying to procure five acres of land in Dehradun, North India, to start a training center and that we needed fifty thousand dollars for that. He graciously gave a check for five thousand dollars, one-tenth of the total required, though he himself had financial struggles as the pastor of a new congregation that was being birthed.

On the following Monday morning, June 23, while driving me to the airport, Pastor Steve told me we must make a model of the college we are trying to build in India. He told me something like this:

> *"American people have to see things to get excited about anything. Make a model that you can show people. That would create interest in more people."*

I told him I had no idea what we would build as we had no funds and might be constructing just one or two rooms to start the ministry. His reply was:

> *"Don't worry whether you have money or not. Just sit and dream and make a model of all you need. You*

need classrooms, a library, dormitories, etc. Make a model of the whole campus."

When I got back to Los Angeles, I called Pastor Herb and conveyed what Pastor Steve said. Immediately Pastor Herb affirmed that it was a great idea. He asked me to meet him in his office right away. By the time I drove out to Culver City, Pastor Herb had already called two young people to his office- Karl Mantl, an architect, and Craig Reynolds[62], a graphic artist.

The way Karl met Pastor Herb and became a member of the church is another evidence of God's sovereign grace. Karl was born and raised in a nominal Roman Catholic family in Austria. His father owned a large construction company in Europe. So, Karl developed an interest in architecture at a young age, studied architecture in Austria, and worked as an architect there before migrating to the US in 1984. He was working as an architect in Los Angeles and was living with his girlfriend. After a while, they decided to get married. Though he was a non-practicing Roman Catholic, he felt that he must get married in a church. So, he looked in the Los Angeles Yellow Pages and "stumbled upon" West Los Angeles Christian Center![63]

When Karl asked Pastor Herb to bless his marriage, Pastor told Karl that he and his fiancé must attend several marriage counseling sessions with him before he would conduct the wedding. In the process of counseling, Pastor

---

[62] Craig is the one who gave us the "holy hand-shake" when we first went to West LA Christian Center way back in 1975.

[63] Is it just a coincidence that ten years earlier we too had "stumbled upon" the same church through Los Angeles Yellow Pages and ten years later Karl, whom God used to direct us to the "exact place" in India that the Lord had chosen for us? You will see how that happened as our story unfolds.

Herb gave Karl a German Bible as Karl's mother tongue is German. As Karl read the Bible for the first time in his life, the Holy Spirit convicted him that living with his fiancé before being married is wrong. When he told his fiancé that they must stop living together before getting married, she became furious. She gave him an ultimatum: "Choose your Bible or me; you cannot have both." Though Karl loved her very much, he chose God and the Bible. In Karl's own words: *"This was very painful, for I loved her, but the truth in the Word was more powerful and important to follow."* So, Karl, broken-hearted, left his fiancé.

He started attending West Los Angeles Christian Center regularly. Within a few weeks, the Lord spoke to him very clearly through Psalm 115, and Karl was born again. A few months later, Pastor Herb baptized him, and he became an active member of West Los Angeles Christian Center. Thus, when Pastor Herb asked Karl and Craig to build the model, Karl was a relatively new believer in Christ. Both Karl and Craig were more than glad to help. But there was a significant problem. Neither had been to India and did not have any idea about Indian architecture.

We told them that the model was only a fund-raising tool, and therefore, it did not matter how they built it. We are not going to use it to construct the actual buildings in India in any way. Then Karl told me:

> *"Brother George, I want something in the model to be real. I cannot build the model according to Indian architecture. Please describe to me in detail the land you have in India, and I will make a replica of the land in the model."*

That is when Karl realized that we did not even have land! Then he told us something like:

"Okay. I will pray and ask the Lord to show me the land He has prepared for the Bible College in India. And I will make a replica of that."

I did not take Karl very seriously at all. But he was serious. As he started making the model, he prayed and asked the Lord to show him the land He had for us in India. Listen to his own words about how he built the model:

"As I continued working on the model, I kept praying and crying out to God to help in forming the land layout which would be identical to the land in India where the Bible School should be built. After I prayed, I glued the different Styrofoam pieces in place. This was truly amazing. The following day, I began building a hill in the back of the model, which ended up resembling a terrace-style landscape. The rough layout began to materialize within hours."[64]

Because Karl was a very busy architect, it took him a while to finish the model. As I was busy traveling to raise funds needed to purchase the land, Leela and I did not have a chance to see the model.

Karl and Craig heard that we would be attending the convention in Redondo Beach in October and wanted to surprise us. They placed the model in a prominent place in the foyer of the church before the convention began. When we walked in, we were very pleasantly surprised to see the professional model Karl and Craig had made. It was four by four in size. While Karl had made beautiful buildings, trees, and roads, what stood out and instantly captured our attention was how he had made the land's layout. The landscape was unique. While one faced the campus, the land came down to the front in tiers. Then, on the righthand rear corner, Karl had

---

[64] From personal correspondence with Karl Mantle.

built a unique feature- a small mount with staircase-like steps to the top. That mount jumped at me. I could not put it out of my mind. I said to myself that it was just Karl's imagination and did not signify anything. Yet, it kept coming back to me again and again.

The model that Karl Mantl built in Los Angeles.
Craig Reynolds assisted Karl. Notice the knoll on the
righthand corner.

I had booked flight tickets to India for Wednesday, November 5, 1986. On Tuesday evening at about 8 o'clock, Jim called us with excitement in his voice.

> _"George, we got another letter from that lady in Georgia,"_ he said. _"And she wants to give you two hundred thousand dollars to build the college!"_

We told Jim that we would like to see the letter. He took it to Pastor Herb, and we met him and read the letter together. Mrs. New offered a memorial gift if we agreed to name the college in memory of her late husband, Luther W. New Jr.

Immediately, we made calls to all the Board members. There was consensus among all that naming the college was not a problem, provided Mrs. New would give us the freedom to manage the college's affairs without interference from her. The Board asked me to write a letter to Mrs. New thanking her for her offer and informing her that one of the Board members would contact her and negotiate all the details. The Board authorized Rory Starks, one of my colleagues from World Vision, to correspond with Mrs. New.

I wrote the letter on my flight from Los Angeles to New York JFK, posted it in JFK, and flew to India.

Later, when we had the opportunity to spend extended time with Mrs. New, she told us some amazing details of how she decided to give such a significant gift to a person she had never met. All through the story, the faithfulness and sovereignty of the Lord came through loud and clear. He is indeed *Jehovah Jireh*, a faithful God who keeps His promises.

Chapter 15

God Still Speaks!

I felt so excited that I did not need an airplane to fly to India! God had already started to fulfill His promise that He gave us through Mrs. Carol Allen in Roseburg, Oregon. We could not wait to see what awaited us as we began this adventure of faith.

I flew to Kerala to attend the wedding of my brother's firstborn, Omana, on November 10. After attending the marriage, Babu and I traveled to Dehradun. Pastor T.J. Simon, Brother Jacob Chacko, and Brother Narendra Katare have been enquiring about the availability of land in and around Dehradun. They were all waiting for us to come with funds to proceed.

Brother Jacob Chacko went out of his way to help us. Mr. Swain, who promised us that he would get us five acres of land if we came with five hundred thousand Rupees, showed us a three-acre plot and asked us seven hundred and fifty thousand Rupees!

I told Babu about the model Karl Mantl and Craig Reynolds built in Los Angeles and how the little mount in the model struck me as something special. He also took it as a sign from the Lord. From then on, whenever we went to see a property, he would ask me: "Sunnychaya[65], do you see the mount?" Of course, there was no "mount" in any property we

---

[65] "Sunny" is the pet name that my parents gave me. According to our culture older people are never addressed just by their names. Some term of respect is always added to their name. In Malayalam, our mother tongue, the common term is 'Achayan'. When that term is added to "Sunny," it becomes "Sunnychayan" in everyday spoken language. "Sunnychaya" is the vocative form.

saw, and everything was too expensive. We kept praying persistently the same prayer we started in 1984:

> *"Lord, lead us to the exact place that you want us to be in North India."*

Though we looked all over Dehradun and the surrounding areas, we could not locate any property that would suit our needs and one we could afford. One day, I told Babu that Dehradun might not be the place that the Lord has chosen for us and that we might have to look elsewhere as we could not afford to spend more than five hundred thousand Rupees for land.

I had committed to a congregation in Bahrain that I would speak for them during the Christmas holidays. I needed to get to Bahrain by December 22. That date was fast approaching, and we still had not found any property we could acquire.

A Christian family in Dehradun, Mr. and Mrs. Mehrab Massey, was extraordinarily gracious to us. On December 15, 1986, Mrs. Massey, a school teacher, sent one of her assistants with us to introduce us to the Pradhan (Chief) of Kulhan village, a village about ten kilometers away from the city's center.

We reached Kulhan as dusk was approaching. The Pradhan was a tall, distinguished, and gracious elderly gentleman, and he received us very warmly in the little teashop he owned. He immediately served us tea and heard us very attentively. The Lord knit his heart with our hearts and put a special love for us in him. He pledged that he would help us find suitable land to build the school.

Then he led us to a steep bank of a dry riverbed, and pointed to a piece of land on the other side of the riverbed. As it was already dusk, we could not see the land very clearly.

Yet, both Babu and I noticed something tantalizing in the layout of the land and wanted to see it up close.

But, before we could say anything, Brother Jacob Chacko said:

> *"Oh, that is on the other side of the river. Water and electric connection would be difficult there. Let's not go there."*

Since Brother Chacko is a Board member and our gracious host, we did not want to offend him and ask the Pradhan to take us across to the land. So, we turned back and returned home after thanking the elderly gentleman. *Both Babu and I were restless that night because of the unique landscape we saw in the dim light of dusk.*

We were eager to see the land by the daylight. So, we convinced Brother Jacob to drive us out there the next day. We met the Pradhan, and together we walked down to the property. When we reached the near side of the dry riverbed, the Pradhan pointed once again to the land that lay on the other side. Babu did not ask me his usual question. I could not believe my eyes. ***If I did not know any better, I would have thought that Karl Mantl stood where we were standing when he made his model in Los Angeles!*** The land, as we saw from that vantage point, came down to us in tiers. ***On the righthand rear corner was this unique mount with steps on it, almost like a staircase.*** Babu and I looked at each other in amazement, and we both ran and climbed on the knoll. The Pradhan and others with us had no idea why we were so excited and why we were running. On top of the small mount, we were praising God and thanking Him, having an old-fashioned revival time while the others in the group caught up with us!

We asked the Pradhan how large the land was. He replied that it was a little over five acres.

"What is the price?" we asked with excitement. *"I do not know,"* he replied. *"If you are interested in the property, I will be glad to introduce you to the owner."* *"Yes, we are,"* we replied.

The property owner was Dr. V.K. Goyal, a Hindu medical doctor who had a clinic in downtown Dehradun. We drove down to the city and went directly to his house and met him. We asked him whether the land was still for sale, and he answered in the affirmative. *"What is the price?"* Dr. Goyal asked us such a low price that we could not believe our ears.

Let me explain. The standard unit of land measurement in Dehradun is "biga." Five "bigas" make an acre. Up to that point, the lowest asking price for a biga that anyone had asked us was twenty thousand Rupees. Some had asked us as much as thirty and forty thousand Rupees. Dr. Goyal asked us for ten thousand Rupees!

So, we bluntly asked him why it was such a low price. He was a sincere man. He smiled and told us this amazing story.

His father had purchased the land several years ago to convert it into a mango orchard, as mango orchards are all around there. Even though Dr. Goyal's father worked hard and planted mango trees again and again, they all kept dying. Only about two dozen trees took root in the 5 acres plus land. Even those trees were sickly and were not growing healthy.

So, he gave up his plans. The family then thought they would get the zoning changed and sell the land as no one would buy an agricultural property in which not even mango trees would grow. Dr. Goyal tried to get the zoning changed to no avail. He was desperate to sell it to expand his clinic and had been trying to sell it for a long time and could not find any buyers. So, he had reduced the asking price.

Land as we saw first. Notice the staircase-like knoll on the right-hand rear corner. Notice also the sparsely growing mango trees.

We asked him whether he would be willing to enter into a contingency agreement with the understanding that we would purchase the land if we got the necessary permits to build the training center. He was more than glad. So, we got the help of one of the best attorneys in Dehradun, Mr. Jitendra Kumar, to write the contingency agreement. The terms of the deal were that we would give fifty thousand Rupees as a down payment and that Dr. Goyal would return the money with simple interest if we did not get the necessary permits to build on the land.

We also hired the services of a well-known architect in the city, Mr. C. B. Narang, to draw up preliminary plans for a college campus and apply for the zoning change, sealing change[66], and building permits. We submitted all the applications to the city planning authority and set a six-month deadline trusting that if it is the Lord's perfect will, He will work for us.[67]

We surveyed the land, and it was 5.9 acres. In answer to the prayers of Leela and the other saints of West LA Christian Center, the Lord gave us 5.9 acres for twenty-five thousand dollars, including all legal expenses, according to the exchange rate of the time! Though the prayer was only for five acres, the answer was 5.9 acres! Is that not how our Lord works? He gives us more than we ask.

When I showed the photographs of the land to Karl, he could not believe his eyes. Even though he prayed and

---

[66] Sealing change refers to a permit to purchase more than a customarily permitted land area.

[67] The red tape of India is notorious. While there has been a lot of improvement in the bureaucracy in the country in recent years, in the 80s, it would take years to get anything moving through the system unless a lot of bribes were given. God sovereignly helped us to overcome all those difficulties.

asked the Lord to show him the land He had for us in India, Karl did not realize that God was speaking through him. He was just a newborn baby in Christ. Yet, God spoke through him. Our God is living, and He still speaks, even through newborn Christians. Only those who have ears to hear, hear God as it has been from the very beginning.

Chapter 16

Vision Becomes a Reality

Dr. Goyal gladly signed the contingency agreement. Soon Mr. Narang drew up plans for the campus and submitted all the needed applications to Mussoorie Dehradun Development Authority (MDDA) for the zoning change, sealing change, and building permits all at once.

We kept praying that all the necessary permits would come through if it was the place that the Lord had chosen for us. Before the six-month deadline that we had set expired, all the needed permits came through. On July 21, 1987, Steve Woodworth, my boss from World Vision, broke grounds to start construction of the campus. All the founding Board members of Bharat Susamachar Samiti, under the leadership of our Chairman, Rev. C. George, and several Christian leaders from various denominational backgrounds, attended the groundbreaking ceremony.

Groundbreaking, July 21, 1987. I am in the middle.
Our younger son, Renny, is the boy standing behind me.

July 21, 1987, is celebrated as the Foundation Day of the Luther W. New Jr. Theological College, commonly known as New Theological College or NTC. On that day, our good friend and my former boss, during my World Vision days, Steve Woodworth, broke the ground to start construction of the campus.

Foundation work. Notice the knoll with steps behind.

Neither Babu nor I had any experience in building anything. To two total novices, the Lord entrusted the task of constructing not just one building but a whole campus. We both were utterly inadequate to undertake the responsibility. In His mercy, our good Lord gave Babu the spirit of wisdom, just like He gave wisdom and skills to Bezalel and Oholiab to construct the Tabernacle.

In constructing the campus, we learned another spiritual principle: *when the Lord calls us to do anything, He equips us. He does not leave us on our own. If we remain dependent on Him and not lean on our understanding or abilities, He will provide the right people and the resources to complete the task.*

The promises in Proverbs 3:5 and 6 are indeed true.

"Trust in the LORD with all your heart

and lean not on your own understanding;

in all your ways submit to him,

and he will make your paths straight."

A God Who Makes Crooked Paths Straight for His Children:

As stated earlier, Mrs. Janie Fountain New wrote in her second letter that she would give two hundred thousand dollars as a memorial gift to construct the college in her late husband's name. Several people worked hard to discourage her from providing the funds when the news got out. As she told us in person later, several well-meaning saints told her we would steal the money. After all, she had not even met us and knew nothing about us. How can she trust a person about whom she knew nothing?

Moreover, there are plenty of proven stories of Christian leaders' unfaithfulness in India. Several people told her such stories. One person told her: *"Janie, you are putting your money down a rat-hole. This man will steal all of it."[68]* We have no ill feelings for anyone who told Mrs. New to be cautious and not to trust us. The untrustworthiness of so many so-called servants of God justified such caution. Another strategy some others used to discourage her from giving was pointing out that I was a Pentecostal. How can a Southern Baptist believer support a Pentecostal? Why not give to a Southern Baptist cause?

---

[68] Mrs. New's personal report to us.

Mrs. New had almost reached the point of writing a letter to us withdrawing her pledge because of all this. At the same time, she also felt compelled in her spirit to keep her promise. She strongly felt that the Lord directed her to help us to build the training center. As she was thinking and praying for God's guidance and direction, an idea came to her. She decided to go to her Pastor and seek his counsel. Her Pastor at that time was Dr. Al Meredith.[69] He is a man of God who is broadminded. He did not think I was disqualified for the gift simply because I was not a Southern Baptist. He also promised Mrs. New that he would check me out.

Once again, God's providence and sovereignty had prepared the path before us. Pastor Al told Mrs. New that he has a dear friend who works in World Vision and that he would call him and ask him about me. It just so happened that his friend knew me well and was a dear friend to me! When Dr. Meredith called him, Jim gave a very positive report about me and told him that I am one hundred percent trustworthy and that there is no need to worry. Not only did he provide an excellent recommendation to Dr. Meredith, he immediately went to Dr. Ted Engstrom, President of World Vision International, and informed him that a lady in Georgia wanted to help us and that she was being discouraged by several people.

---

[69] Dr. Al Meredith was the senior pastor of Frist Baptist Church, Elberton, Georgia, the congregation that Mrs. New was a member of. I was blessed to meet him in 1987 when I visited Mrs. New for the first time. Dr. Meredith graciously invited me to preach at First Baptist Church. He left Elberton in 1988 to become the senior pastor of Wedgewood Baptist Church, Ft. Worth, Texas, and served that congregation for almost twenty-seven years. That church was the scene of a mass shooting on September 14, 1999, in which seven church members were killed and seven more were wounded. In 2019, he published *Surviving Catastrophe: Lessons Learned from the Wedgwood Shooting*.

As soon as Dr. Ted heard it, he picked up the phone and called Mrs. New in person and assured her of our integrity. Dr. Ted also told her that if she had any concerns at all, to give funds to World Vision and that World Vision would make sure that the college would be built and named after her husband. When Mrs. New heard from Dr. Ted, her doubts vanished. The excellent report that my friend Jim gave to Dr. Meredith added to her confidence.

She gave the first hundred thousand dollars to World Vision, and World Vision gave the funds to Good News for India. By the time she was ready to donate the second hundred thousand, we had met, and she had enough confidence to give the funds directly to us. She and her sister, Mrs. Lucille Holliman, ended up giving altogether over six hundred and fifty thousand dollars for the Lord's work in India. Praise God for God's children who give generously for His Kingdom!

You see how God placed the right people in critical places to fulfill His plan and purpose. If her Pastor was a narrow-minded person, he could easily have persuaded Mrs. New not to give to a Pentecostal. If Jim were not my colleague, there would not have been an opportunity for Dr. Al Meredith to check me out, and Dr. Ted would never have heard about people discouraging Mrs. New from giving to us.

God orchestrated everything in such a beautiful way, and He fulfilled His purposes. All glory to Him alone! Because of Mrs. New's gift, we finished constructing the first phase of the campus without any financial difficulties.

April 15, 1989, Dedication Day:

It took well over a year to complete the first phase of construction. On April 15, 1989, Dr. Ted Engstrom, President-Emeritus, World Vision International, and Rev. Orvel Taylor, President, Christian Evangelistic Assemblies (now Grace International), dedicated the college. Mrs. Janie Fountain New, the widow of Luther W. New Jr., in whose memory the college is named, unveiled the stone of dedication. Mrs. New was 81 years old. Her 83-year-old sister, Mrs. Lucille Holliman, also attended the dedication ceremony.

Over twenty friends and well-wishers from the US, including Mrs. Orvel Taylor, Rev. Marvin Bell and his daughter Debbi Bell, Rev. and Mrs. Paul Adams, and Rev. Timothy Tennent, then a pastor in Georgia and now the President of Asbury Theological Seminary, also took part in the dedication service.

Over two hundred Indian Christian leaders also were present during the joyous occasion. Right after the dedication service, Dr. Engstrom taught his well-known course on Christian Leadership and Time Management to sixty specially invited Christian leaders from all over India.

Thus, the Lord fulfilled our dream of starting *a small* training center in North India far more gloriously than we ever thought possible.

My wife and I often tell each other that we would have been the biggest fools if we neglected the call of God and held on to our jobs and the comfortable life-style of Southern California. How many miracles we would have missed!

Because God gave us the grace to obey Him now, we have over three thousand "children" who are serving the Lord all over the world. To see the glory of God we must believe, we must obey! There is no faith where there is no obedience. May the Lord give us His grace to continue to trust Him and obey Him even when the cost of obedience might look like too much!

The Luther W. New Jr. Theological College (NTC) Campus, Dehradun, India, when it was dedicated on April 15, 1989, by Dr. Ted Engstrom, President-Emeritus, World Vision, and Rev. Orvel Taylor, President, CEA.

Dr. Ted Engstrom, President Emeritus, World Vision, delivered the dedication message.

Chapter 17

Pioneering Creative Ways of Training.

Dr. Victor Choudhary's Challenge

When the first phase of the campus construction was going on, we continued our travel, seeking counsel from concerned leaders on how best to serve the Church in North India. We did not want to confine our training programs to the traditional theological Seminary/Bible College model. While the conventional training model has contributed significantly to the Church's leadership in India, that model alone cannot produce enough laborers for the Lord's vineyard.

Slowly, God opened our minds to see that a strategically placed training center with a vision to reach as many of the unreached people as possible with the Gospel needs to train people at *many different levels* to meet the needs that such a large subcontinent presents.

One of the critical figures God used to guide us in this direction is Dr. Victor Choudhary, former Director of Christian Medical College, Ludhiana, Punjab. We met him in CMC, Ludhiana, during our travel through North India. One of the first questions he asked challenged us.

"Do you know how many native-born Punjabi Christians are there with a Batchelor of Divinity degree (BD)?", he asked.

I could not answer him as I had no idea at all. After a long silence, he replied: *"None!"*

That shocked us. He went on to explain the reason.[70] Many Punjabi Christians who have a call to Christian ministry do not have the opportunity for higher education. Even many bright Punjabi Christian youths have to stop their education with 10th class or, at most, with 12th due to economic difficulties. As a result, the Church of North India, the Methodist Church, and other mainline Protestant denominations must depend on candidates from other parts of the country to have ordained clergymen, as the minimum qualification for ordination is a BD degree. For a young person to apply for admission to BD, he must have a bachelor's degree.[71]

Very few Punjabi Christian young people who have received a call for ministry have had the opportunity to pursue a University education. Dr. Choudhary challenged us to do what we can to help such young people. He argued that we must not confine ourselves exclusively to theological education, nor should we be satisfied by offering a basic Bible School level training. We must think of contributing to the academic upliftment of the poor Christians as we plan the institution we hoped to build, he counseled us.

For sure, the Lord had ordained the time that we spent with Dr. Choudhary. His wisdom helped us to pioneer an educational experiment that ended up helping scores of young people.

As we parted company, he told us to let him know once we were ready to admit students and that he would supply ample applicants. And he kept his promise. Large

---

[70] This was in 1987. Praise God that the situation has changed. There are many Punjabi Christian youth with advanced theological degrees now.

[71] The Serampore College (University) has recently started an integrated BD course for which a high school graduate can seek admission.

numbers of the trainees for the first several batches of the Discipleship Training Courses in NTC came from Punjab directly because of Dr. Choudhary.

Later, Dr. Choudhary himself told us how that happened. Many young Punjabi Christians would apply for jobs in CMC. When he interviews them, Dr. Choudhary would ask them to recite the Lord's Prayer or Psalm 23 or some other simple Bible passage. Though they were Christians, coming from Christian homes, none could recite even the Lord's prayer accurately! Then he would tell them to go and study for six months in the new Bible College at Dehradun and come back and apply again for the job. As a result, scores of young people came to NTC. They hoped that they would get a good job at CMC if they completed the six-month course in NTC. They were not coming to study the Bible or because they loved Jesus! Their motive was a job at CMC!

Several of the young people who came gave us real hard times as they were not born again and had no sense of call on their lives. Some of them sneaked out of the dormitories at night to smoke and get drunk! They got into fights with one another. They were purely worldly people whose ambition was to somehow complete the six-month course and go back to Dr. Choudhary, get a job in the prestigious medical college, and make a decent living!

But God had other plans for them! As part of the training, we focused very much on fasting, prayer, and waiting on the Lord. We spent long periods of time for worship. During those glorious times of worship, the presence of the Lord came down in extraordinary ways. None of these young people had ever been in such an atmosphere before. As a result, before the course was over, every one of those people personally experienced the touch of the Holy Spirit and were born again and called into ministry! Lord Jesus radically transformed their lives. Not one went back to

154

CMC to ask for a job! Everyone went back to their native places in Punjab and started churches and other ministries.

Dr. Choudhary has told us many humorous stories about seeing some of these young people later. He said he tried to avoid meeting them, thinking that they would pester him for a job because he had promised that he would consider them for employment if they would complete the training in NTC. To his surprise, not one he saw asked him for a job. Instead, everyone invited Dr. Choudhary to his Church to preach! He has narrated beautiful stories of going and speaking to large numbers of people worshipping the Lord under tree shades and temporary shelters, all organized by the helter-skelter gang that he sent to NTC for training! So, he kept sending more and more young people for training to NTC, both to the six months DTC course and to the longer degree course.

These victory stories from the early days of NTC encouraged us to press on even more boldly to expand our training programs.

Mission Orientation Course.

Our passion has always been to motivate all believers to obey the Great Commission of our Lord.[72] We sincerely believe that the Great Commission is the "job description" of the Church. Why else would He leave the Church on this earth? The Lord has left His Bride, the Church on this earth, to "make disciples of all nations."

The word translated "nations" is the Koine Greek word "ethne," from which we get the English word "ethnic" and related words.[73] While the current English word "nations"

---

[72] Matthew 28:18-20 and parallels. Great Commission is given seven times in the New Testament!

[73] ἔθνος (ethnos) is singular and ἔθνη (ethne) is plural.

gives us the idea of political entities such as "the nation of India" or "the nation of Pakistan", the Biblical meaning is very different from that. When John Wycliffe translated the Bible into English in 1382 and William Tyndale in 1525, the word "nation" did convey the idea of "ethnic group" and not what it means today. We are convinced that God's desire has always been to bless "all the families of the earth" (מִשְׁפָּחָה mishpachah) as he promised Abraham in Genesis 12:3. The New Testament word "ethnos/ethne" conveys the same sense of the Hebrew word "mishpachah" in Genesis 12:3. Almost all Indian languages translate "ethnos/ethne" with the word "jathi," which accurately conveys the Biblical meaning. India has 4,693 "jathi" ("nations"), and a vast number of these are still waiting for adequate Gospel witness.

We emphasized the Church's responsibility to reach the unreached with the Gospel from the very beginning. Starting a "Mission Orientation Course" was a visible expression of our inner conviction. God used this course to challenge many young people to commit themselves to reaching the unreached.

"Double Degree Program."

We were praying for the Lord's direction to show us how to respond to Dr. Choudhary's plea to help poor Christian youth who do not have an opportunity for higher education. God gave us the idea of what later came to be known as a "double degree program." It has helped scores of young people since we launched the program in 1991.

This innovative program solved two issues for us. NTC had no accreditation when we launched the degree course, Bachelor of Theology (B.Th.) in 1991. We had no library or enough qualified faculty members. I did not want anyone to spend three or four years of her/his young life with us and then end up with a piece of paper (a diploma or a degree) with no value. Several so-called Bible Colleges in

156

India were doing that, and some are still doing it. We would not want our sons or daughters to study in an institution that has no academic credibility. I felt that same responsibility to the young people who committed to spending precious years of their lives in NTC.

The "double degree program" solved that issue for us in a beautiful way. We would coach the students and present them to the Indira Gandhi National Open University (IGNOU). When they met all the requirements, they got a universally recognized degree from IGNOU. They also received a Bachelor of Theology degree from NTC. So, all who were willing to work hard and had academic talents received two degrees simultaneously: one degree in theology from NTC and another from IGNOU in the discipline of their choice, such as Economics, English, History, or Sociology.[74]

We are very grateful to the Lord for His grace and mercy in leading us by hand every step of the way and to Dr. Victor Choudhary for challenging us to think in creative ways. This foundation has helped several talented NTC graduates to earn master's and doctoral degrees from prestigious institutions without wasting precious years of their lives. The "double degree program" has also enabled several NTC graduates to become fully qualified primary and secondary school teachers. We give all glory to God for directing our steps in pioneering this unique program and express our sincere thanks to Dr. Victor Chaudhary for his far-sightedness in challenging us to think in creative ways.

---

[74] A few years later, when our older son, Finny, received admission to Harvard University as a national merit scholar for a double doctorate (MD/Ph.D.), one of our colleagues in NTC, Brother Sudheer Kurup, called me aside and told me that it was the Lord's reward for us for helping scores of poor young people in North India to do "double degree!" That was very kind of him to think that way. We are glad that this innovative course has greatly helped many young people. All glory to God!

Chapter 18

God Gathers An Amazing Team

The most critical element in any enterprise is people. Without the right team, no one can accomplish anything, whether it is for the Lord's Kingdom or for a secular business.

While the Lord's initial call came to Leela and me, the first couple that the Lord united with us was Babu and Laly (Rev. and Mrs. George C. Kuruvilla). Babu is my only sister's second son.

He and his best childhood friend, K J Kuriakose, had reached Varanasi (aka Banaras), the famous Hindu holy city on the banks of the river Ganges, on July 13, 1976, right after completing their 12th grade. They both received a missionary call from the Lord in high school and wanted to prepare themselves for ministry in North India. God opened the doors for them to study at New Life Bible College, which was led by Rev. K. V. Abraham, Leela's first cousin. It is Rev. Abraham, whom we call Babychayan, who took Leela to Nepal in 1969 and procured her a job as a school teacher in Kathmandu. Later, he moved to Varanasi to lead New Life League ministries.

After completing their studies at New Life Bible College, Babu and Kuriakose served as missionaries with the New Life League in Varanasi and surrounding places. Thus, when the Lord brought us to North India in 1986, Babu was already a missionary there for several years.

Like Epaphroditus, Apostle Paul's companion (see Philippians 3:25 to 27), Babu almost lost his life in serving the Lord with the New Life League. In 1979, he became so seriously ill that doctors gave up hope for his survival. They told the leaders of the Mission to inform his parents and other kith and kin to come and see him right away if they wanted to see him alive. God, in His mercy, touched him and healed him because He had greater things for Babu to do.

In early 1986, God moved in their hearts to leave New Life League as Babu and Laly felt that God had something new for them to do for the Kingdom. So, with the blessing of Rev. K.V. Abraham, they left for Kerala, their native place, and waited on the Lord for their next assignment. There Babu was diagnosed with TB. He was diagnosed and treated by my cousin, the first physician in our family, Dr. Thankamma, whom we endearingly called *Dr. Thankammamma.* Hers was the only hospital near our village, and all the surrounding communities depended on her for their medical needs. It was while he was recuperating from TB under her care that we asked him whether he would consider joining us in North India.

Babu and Laly waited on the Lord and sought His will. And the Lord directed them to join us. Praise God! He was a twenty-eight-year-old when he joined us.

Both Babu and I were "green" in every respect of the word and were least qualified to pioneer a theological seminary and a church-planting ministry. Babu had an advantage over me in that he was very fluent in Hindi and knew the North Indian culture far better than me. He also had almost a decade of missionary experience in North India. But neither of us had constructed anything or established even a small ministry. Looking back over three and a half decades, we can say without any hesitation that the Lord anointed Babu in an exceptional way, just as He anointed Bezalel, Oholiab, and other skilled workers to build the Tabernacle. (See Exodus 31:1-11.)

Leela and I express our heartfelt gratitude and thanks to Babu and Laly for all the sacrifices they made and for all their hard work. Without them, none of the things we have accomplished in ministry would have become a reality. We are eternally grateful to the Lord for uniting their hearts with ours and for enabling us to work together all these years without any serious conflicts between us. All glory to God and sincere, heartfelt thanks to Babu and Lalamma, as we call them.

God also knew that the four of us alone could not accomplish His purpose in calling us. So, He began to move in the hearts and minds of other like-minded brothers and sisters, brought them to us, and blessed us with a great team from the beginning.

One of the first ones to join the team was A. G. Jude, who graduated from Doon Bible College with a Bachelor of Theology degree (B.Th.) in 1987. He joined us right after his graduation. He was a great help to Babu as we started the campus construction on July 21, 1987.

Jude got married to Jayamol (Suja) the following year, and thus, we became three families. Jayamol, also hailing from Kerala, was working in the Landour Community Hospital, a Christian Mission hospital in Mussoorie, a city situated at seven thousand feet in the foothills of the Himalayas. Eventually, God opened the door for Jude to do his theological education. First, he completed his Bachelor of Divinity degree from NTC while working as part of the team. Then, we sponsored his Master of Theology studies at Gurukul Theological Seminary in Tamil Nadu. Jayamol worked in the Principal's office until she retired recently. Jude continues to teach in the Department of Theology.

Along with Jude, Benjamin Paul, and Reji John, both graduates of DBC, joined us for church-planting work, as that has been our passion from the beginning. Reji John continues to serve with us as a senior pastor and leader. Benjamin Paul is a prominent pastor in Dehradun and is currently pastoring one of the oldest congregations in the area, the Masihi Mandli.

We only had a motor scooter in those days for transportation. We rented a house about six kilometers away from the land the Lord gave us and where campus construction was planned. Babu, Laly, their two children-Benjamin and Daniel- and Jude lived in that house with me whenever I was in the country. On October 4, 1990, Barnabas, the youngest of Babu and Laly, was born.

Through Babu's influence, his best friend, K. J. Kuriakose, and his wife, Molamma, joined us on January 2nd, 1991. His joining strengthened the team significantly. As he did not have an accredited theological degree, we encouraged him to pursue a Bachelor of Divinity (BD) and later a Master of Theology (M.Th.) degree. KJK, as he is commonly known, served faithfully with us until he was called to pastor a congregation in Oklahoma in 2009. He served as the President of CEA and as a Professor of Christian Ministry when he took up pastoral responsibilities in the US. We miss his valuable leadership even after all these years.

My cousin, The Rev. C. George, who served as the Chairman of our Board, was instrumental in persuading several key people to join us as we were unknown to most of the Indian Christian community. His leadership in the early days was vital in team building. Through his influence, a young couple, M.D. Abraham and his wife, Sarah, joined us. They contributed immensely in the early years of NTC. Another important person who joined through "Uncle" C. George's influence was Mr. Kurian Thomas. He had many years of teaching and administrative experience in Zambia, Africa. He helped us immensely in administration during the early years.

Yet another couple recruited by "Uncle" C. George is Simon Samuel and Mercy. We cannot describe in words the contribution of this couple in making NTC what it is today. They also joined us in 1991 after completing his MTh studies in New Testament at United Theological College Bangalore. In 1995, God opened the door for them to pursue doctoral studies in the United Kingdom. After completing his Ph.D. in New Testament from Sheffield University, United Kingdom, they returned to India. It is particularly noteworthy that Mercy, a registered nurse, worked in the United Kingdom National Health Service (NHS) and financially supported Simon's studies. They could easily have stayed in the UK after his studies. But instead, they chose to return to North India to serve the Lord.

Dr. Samuel became the Principal of NTC in 2004 and served till July 2023, when he stepped down and became Principal Emeritus. Under his competent and dedicated leadership, NTC became what it is today, one of the most influential theological seminaries in India.

Through my brother-in-law, Mr. P.C. Kuruvilla, the father of Babu, our first accountant, Mr. Jacob Varghese, joined us and served with us till November 30, 2023.

Through Rev. Mathews Varghese, who is married to my niece, Daisy, and is a senior leader in our church planting work and also serves as the senior pastor of Good News Center, Bhopal, MP, from the early 1980s, we were introduced to Rev. P.B. Thomas, then a lecturer at Faith Theological Seminary, Manakkala, Kerala. As he felt a call to North India and expressed his desire to serve the Lord with us, we helped him with his doctoral studies at Westminster Theological Seminary, Philadelphia. After completing his studies, he joined NTC and assumed the role of Principal on July 1, 1998, and served till April 2002. Under Dr. Thomas's leadership, NTC received its affiliation with the Serampore College (University).

We are grateful to him and his wife, Mrs. Vimala Thomas, who also served as a faculty member with us. Through the influence of Rev. P.B. Thomas, Dr. Joseph Abraham joined the team in 1996 and served till April 2002.

Over time, two more of Babu's friends who served with him in Varanasi joined us: T.S. Sam and P.V. Joseph. God opened the door for them to pursue higher studies at Gordon Conwell Theological Seminary. P. V. Joseph completed his Ph.D. studies at Boston University and is currently serving as Professor of Theology at NTC. T. S. Sam retired in 2016.

Another two key persons that the Lord miraculously brought to us are Mr. Varghese Samuel and his wife, Molamma. We call Mr. Samuel, Babykutty. We are from the same village. We have known each other since childhood. He is almost ten years younger than me. He used to attend the children's club that I organized as a teenager (See page 39).

He married Molamma, a registered nurse, and they were serving in the Oasis Mission hospital in Al Ain, the United Arab Emirates. He was an Assistant Administrator in the hospital. They were married for many years and had no children, though they sought expert medical help from many physicians, including a top specialist in Indianapolis, USA. They spent considerable time in Indianapolis seeking medical help to have a child. That doctor told them that it was humanly impossible for them to have a child. Only God could do it!

They knew the Lord's call was upon them for ministry, yet they hesitated to step out. Once they realized they would not have a child, they prayed together and decided to resign from their jobs and enroll in Union Biblical Seminary (UBS), Poona, to prepare for full-time ministry.

A few months into their studies at UBS, Molamma became ill. Though doctors examined her several times, they could not diagnose anything wrong with her. Then, someone suggested that they do a pregnancy test. To their utter surprise, they found out that she was indeed pregnant!

When they obeyed the call on their lives and stepped out in faith, God did what man thought was impossible! They named the beautiful daughter that the Lord gave them Saramol. She is a vibrant young lady now married and walking with the Lord. God's deeds are indeed marvelous.

Once they completed their training at UBS, they joined our team and served for many years with NTC and CEA, our church-planting ministry. He served as the President of CEA until his father's health failed, and he needed to return to Kerala to care for him. Even then, whenever he could, he would come up to North and serve the Lord with us.

Another key couple that the Lord brought to us is John Davidson and his wife, Sheba. They joined the team in September 1993 and served till May 2004. Brother Davidson served as the Principal of NTC between the tenure of Dr. P B Thomas and Dr. Simon Samuel. NTC benefitted greatly from the selfless service of both. We are grateful to them and still miss them very much in the team.

There are many other leaders that the Lord brought to the team over time. Time and space limitations prevent me from sharing about all of them. A particular joy for us is seeing young men and women who come to NTC with very limited or no knowledge of English blossom and become eloquent preachers and efficient leaders. Several have gone on to complete doctoral degrees both from within India and abroad.

We are very proud that a few of our graduates, such as Rev. Johnson Abraham, Mr. Kedalung Chawang, Dr. Joel Joseph, (Dr.) Jison Saju Joseph, Rev. A.G. Jude, Dr. M.I. Kuriakose, Rev. Santhosh Lukose and his wife Jessy Santhosh, Mrs. Parul Kuruvilla, Dr. Shivraj Mahendra, Mrs. Sheena Oommen, Rev. Sooraj Pal, Dr. Clara Shiju, and Rev. Alex Sreedharan are now faculty members of NTC! All glory to God alone!

What began as a very small institution with a tiny vision has now become one of the largest theological seminaries affiliated to the Senate of Serampore and accredited by ATA. We are now offering up to doctoral level courses. It is the result of so many of God's children working very hard and sacrificing so much. May the Lord who knows the hearts and motives of all bless and reward each one who worked sincerely, sacrificing their personal ambitions! We are confident that the Lord will because he has promised: *". . . now the LORD declares. . . those who **honor** me I will honor…"*1 Samuel 2:30.

From an unproductive mango orchard, God created "a seedbed"[75] that has now trained well over three thousand people for the ministry of the Gospel. We give all glory to God. We also thank everyone who has stood with us, prayed for us, and sacrificially helped us. Blessings!

I am closing the story of God's faithfulness in our lives and ministries here for the time being. If the Lord gives me the opportunity, I will narrate the rest of the story in another volume. If I do not have a chance to do that, I pray that someone else will take it up after I am with the Lord!

Following are glimpses of the campus of the Luther W. New Jr. College (NTC), Dehradun, India. I share these for God's glory.

---

[75] The word "Seminary" comes from the Latin word *"seminarium,"* *which means "seedbed."*

The Center of our Campus is the Janie Fountain New Library.

God has blessed us with a beautiful campus.
In the foreground: Dormitories.

"Jyothiralayam"- House of Light
Where the Word of God is Taught.

Institute of Languages and Linguistics: Training Translators to
Reach All Languages with God's Word.

168

Women have an Important Role in Reaching the Unreached: Our Women's Hostel

Worship and Prayer are top priorities for us. Our Chapel is at the Center of the Campus.

Student body in front of the library

A scene of worship in our chapel.

In addition to the Bible College/Seminary, we have eight primary and secondary schools through which we serve nearly 4,000 children and their families. Most of our schools are called Khrist Jyoti Academy (Light of Christ Academy).

Khrist Jyoti Academy, Pathri, Haridwar *(Estd: 1991)*

Khrist Jyoti Academy, Bhagwanpur, Haridwar *(Estd: 2004)*

Mount Carmel Christian Academy, Narendra Nagar *(Estd: 1997)*

Khrist Jyoti Academy, Dehradun *Estd: 2009*

Khrist Jyoti Academy, Dehradun, High School Building.

Our newly built school in Bihar.

Currently, construction is going on for the school building in Rudraprayg (a collage of students and teachers is below).

Khrist Jyoti Academy, Rudra Prayag. *(Estd: 2006)*

We also have three child care projects through which we serve nearly 500 needy children. These projects are known as **Jeevan Jyoti (Light of Life) Projects.**

174

In addition to the above-mentioned ministries, Lord helped us to pioneer Christian Evangelistic Assemblies of India (CEA). The story of CEA India also needs to be written as a separate account as time and space do not permit me to narrate it here. We are blessed to have hundreds of faithful coworkers who labor with CEA for the Lord. These men and women have pioneered several hundred congregations in seventeen states of India and the country of Nepal. Many of them have suffered much for the cause of the Gospel. We are honored to have them as our coworkers and we salute them.

I often feel that when we stand in front of the Lord to receive our rewards, most of them will receive far greater rewards than I as they have suffered more for the Gospel and worked harder than I. Thank you brothers and sisters for your faithfulness. May the Lord continue to bless you all in every way!

****

The following are two Bible studies that have greatly influenced me. Therefore, I am including these as part of our story. I learned the lessons I am sharing from many Bible teachers. Nothing I share is original to me. I have tried my best to acknowledge all from whom I learned these lessons. I ask pardon as I am sure that I have left out some sources. It is not done purposefully; just because of "senior moments" also known as forgetfulness!

Please read and be blessed.

Chapter 19

God's Purpose in Calling Each of Us

Is there a purpose for our lives? Are we just accidents? Or, as Shakespeare has said, is

"Life's but a walking shadow, a poor player, that struts and frets his hour upon the stage, and then is heard no more; it is a tale told by an idiot, full of sound and fury, signifying nothing."?[76]

Not if the Holy Bible is the infallible Word of God. The Bible teaches that God created every human being in His image for a purpose. Not one is *"a tale told by an idiot, full of sound and fury, signifying nothing."* No one is an accident. Every one of us is *created* for a purpose.

According to Paul the Apostle, the purpose of God is eternal.[77] Jeremiah says that God's purpose is unchanging.[78] Isaiah affirms that God's purpose is immutable.[79] What, then, is God's purpose for you and me?

I believe that answering this question is one of the Holy Bible's central themes: from the first sentence to the last, from the creation narrative, and in every episode after that.

---

[76] Macbeth *(1606) act 5, sc. 5, l. 16*

[77] Ephesians 3:11.

[78] Jeremiah 4:28.

[79] Isaiah 14:24.

Let's begin with Abram/Abraham's history, which illustrates it as best as any other anecdote in the Bible.

We encounter Abram for the first time in the Holy Bible in Genesis 11:26, where we read: *"When Terah had lived 70 years, he fathered Abram, Nahor, and Haran."*

Abram was the youngest son of Terah, who lived in the "Ur of the Chaldeans" (Genesis 11:28, 31; 15:7; Nehemiah 9:7; Acts 7:2-3), an ancient city in modern-day Iraq.[80] Archaeologists have excavated Ur. It was a well-developed city with houses having indoor plumbing in BC 4000!

---

[80] Many casual readers of the Bible might think Abram was the oldest son of Terah because he is mentioned first in his sons' list. However, a careful reading of Genesis will show that he is the youngest. From Genesis 12:4, we know that when Abram left Haran, he was 75 years old. Assuming he left Haran the same year his father died, we can say that Abram was 75 when Terah died. We also know that Terah was 205 when he died (Genesis 11:32). If Abram were his firstborn, Abram ought to have been 130 years when he died because Terah was only 70 when his firstborn was born (Genesis 11:26). Hence, we know for sure that he was not the firstborn. Here is a very significant point in God's call of Abram. According to the accepted custom of the East, the firstborn is always more important than any other offspring. Youngest was not considered significant, as is seen in Jesse's story, David's father. When Samuel came to anoint a king for Israel and asked Jesse to call his sons, who did he call? Of course, the oldest first and then the second, and so forth. When God rejected the first seven, Samuel had to ask him: "Are all your sons here?" Then Jesse replied rather sheepishly: "Their remains yet the youngest (or smallest), but behold, he is keeping the sheep." Only at Samuel's insistence did Jesse call David. (See 1 Samuel 16: 6-12). Nevertheless, God called Abram and David the youngest, not Nahor or Eliab the oldest.

The Bible also tells us that Terah and his family worshiped "other gods" (i.e., idols).[81]

We now know through archaeological discoveries that Ur was the city of the moon god "Nanna" (also known as Nannar, Nanna-Suen, Sin or Su'en, Asimbabbar, and Namrasit).[82] Archaeologists have discovered bricks stamped with "Uru," the city's name, and many tablets and buildings with the god Nanna's inscriptions and images. No longer can anyone say in good faith that what the Bible says about Abram/Abraham is a "myth," as liberal scholars used to say. It is not at all an exaggeration to say that archaeology has confirmed the Bible's accuracy and proven liberal scholars wrong again and again.[83]

Nanna was worshipped in many parts of the ancient world, including Haran. By the way, it is crucial to observe that the symbol of "Nanna" is the crescent moon!

---

[81] *"And Joshua said to all the people, 'Thus says the Lord, the God of Israel, 'Long ago, your fathers lived beyond the Euphrates, Terah, the father of Abraham and of Nahor; and they served other gods.'"* Joshua 24:2.

[82] Nanna is the Mesopotamian god of the moon and wisdom and is one of the oldest gods in the Mesopotamian pantheon. He is first mentioned in written documents as early as 3500 BC. His major worship center was the great temple in Ur, and Abram must have been a devotee of Nanna. Nanna is frequently mentioned as the pantheon's chief god in hymns and inscriptions from Ur, dating as far back as the Ur III Period (2047-1750 BC).

[83] Sir Leonard Wooley first excavated Ur in 1922. He discovered "The Great Death Pit," an elaborate grave complex of royal tombs. In one tomb, seventy-three bodies of servants were found arranged in sacrifice around the gorgeously decorated corpse of Queen Puabi! His excavations also discovered a massive three-staged ziggurat (a rectangular stepped tower) built by Ur-Nammu during the beginning of the second millennium BC. The top level was the shrine of Nanna.

What Abram worshipped when the living God chose him was the crescent moon. Is it just a coincidence that two major religions of the world today, though very different in many respects, have this one thing in common: both use the crescent moon symbol?[84]

We now know that Ur was a vast, wealthy city. It became wealthy because of its strategic location where the Tigris and Euphrates ran into the Persian Gulf. Archaeological excavations have shown that Ur enjoyed a very high living standard, unknown elsewhere in the Mediterranean. So, when the Lord called Abram to leave his *"country, your people and your father's household and go to the land I will show you"* (Genesis 12:1), he was forsaking a comfortable lifestyle to obey God. He left life in a luxurious house with indoor plumbing to live in tents. (Hebrews, 11:9). This is true of most who receive a call from the Lord even today. Before anyone can obey the call of God, he/she has to answer this question: *"Am I willing to give up what I consider precious to receive what the Lord has in store for me?"* Abram and Moses and millions who have come after them in salvation history gladly did and continue to do that. We read this truth in Hebrews 11:24-26:

> *"By faith Moses, when he was grown up, refused to be called the son of Pharaoh's daughter, choosing rather to be mistreated with the people of God than to enjoy the fleeting pleasures of sin. He considered the reproach of Christ greater wealth than the*

---

[84] Sir Leonard Wooley discovered many examples of moon-worship in his excavations of Ur, including a large temple dedicated to Nannar (or Nanna). Many of these artifacts can be seen in the British Museum today.

treasures of Egypt, for he was looking to the reward."

When one grasps the worth of the amazing privilege of following the Master, everything else becomes worthless rubbish.[85] The Kingdom is indeed a pearl of great value compared to all other "pearls," which are of no value.[86] Abram was given the grace to forsake a luxurious city that he could see with his physical eyes to live in tents because he saw by faith an enduring city, one "that has foundations, whose designer and builder is God."[87] Obeying God can be done only by grace, whether in the fourth century BC or today, to forsake one's comfortable lifestyle and step out into the unknown. May the Lord open our eyes and give us the wisdom to see what is truly precious in a world where most seek riches that will not endure and fleeting pleasures!

What we read in Joshua 24:2 is affirmed in stories of Jewish traditions. According to one Midrash commentary on Genesis 11:28, Terah had a successful idol-manufacturing business. One day, he entrusted the shop to Abram and went out somewhere. Whenever anyone would come to buy an idol, Abram would ask him: "How old are you?" According to their age, the person would reply "fifty years" or "sixty years." Then Abram would ask him or her, "Why would a fifty-year-old person want to worship something that was made a day or two ago?" The customer

---

[85] *"Indeed, I count everything as loss because of the surpassing worth of knowing Christ Jesus my Lord. For his sake I have suffered the loss of all things and count them as rubbish, in order that I may gain Christ."* Philippians 3:8

[86] Matthew 13:46.

[87] Hebrews 11:10.

would understand the folly of worshiping an idol and walk out of the shop without buying "a god"!

One day, when Abram was watching the shop, a woman came in with a sack of fine flour and wanted to offer it to the idols. Abram had already received the revelation of the living God and could not understand why anyone would desire to offer anything to an idol. Still, he obliged her and offered the fine flour to all the idols in the shop. After that, Abram took a big stick and destroyed all the idols except the biggest one in the shop. He then put the stick in the hand of that biggest idol.

When Terah came back, he saw all the idols broken and his business destroyed. He questioned Abram to find out what happened. Without batting an eye, he told Terah that when the flour was offered to the idols by a woman, each idol wanted to eat it first, and a fight broke out among them, and the biggest idol won! In his anger, Terah chided Abram and asked him: "Are you making fun of me? Do they know anything?" In response, Abram told his father: "I hope your ears can hear what your mouth is speaking!"

Then Terah took Abram and handed him over to Nimrod. There was a debate between Abram and Nimrod, and Abram's logic confounded Nimrod. In anger, Nimrod consigned Abram to the fire god. However, Abram came out unhurt from the fire. Haran, Abram's brother, was there. When questioned by Nimrod, he sided with Abram. Nimrod, in anger, tossed him into the fire, and Haran was injured and died.[88] While the Bible never tells us this story, it is found in the Midrash and the Quran.[89]

---

[88] Midrasch B'reishit Rabbah commentary of Genesis 11:28 "Haran died in the presence of his father Terah in the land of his kindred, in Ur

We know from the Bible that Abram tended to hide the truth to save his skin. At least twice, he lied or told a half-truth. (See Genesis 12:11-12; 20:2 & 12. Note that Isaac, his son, also followed his father's example in Genesis 26:7. Parents, remember that your children will follow your example!)

So, God did not call Abram because he was a perfect man, as some later Jewish writings say. He was an idolater, liar, and a coward. However, God called him, just as he has called us "while we were still sinners" (Romans 5:8). Paul tells us this great truth that God's call is not dependent upon our merits or qualifications; only on His grace.

> *"For consider your calling, brothers: not many of you were wise according to worldly standards, not many were powerful, not many were of noble birth. But God chose what is foolish in the world to shame the wise; God chose what is weak in the world to shame the strong; God chose what is low and despised in the world, even things that are not, to bring to nothing things that are, so that no human being might boast in the presence of God."* [90]

of the Chaldeans." This story is accepted only as a Jewish legend and not as historically accurate by serious scholars.

[89] Quran 21:51-70. The logical explanation of this myth being found in the Quran is that Prophet Mohammed must have heard the story from his Jewish friends and thought it was historically accurate and included in the Quran. Rabbi Hiyya created the original story only in the 2nd century AD.

[90] 1 Corinthians 1:26-29

Let's get it right at the very beginning. No human has ever been saved because he or she was good and righteous. Not even the best among us *deserves* to be called by God. By grace alone, God calls us and chooses us; it is only because of His mercy.

One might wonder: "Was not Enoch a perfect human? Was it not because of his perfection that God took him?" *"Enoch walked with God, and he was not, for God took him."*[91]

Alternatively, what about Noah, of whom it is written: *"Noah was a righteous man, blameless in his generation. Noah walked with God."*?[92]

The writer of Hebrews answers that question for us in 11:5 and 7:

> *"By faith Enoch was taken up so that he should not see death, and he was not found, because God had taken him. Now before he was taken he was commended as having pleased God."*

> *"By faith Noah, being warned by God concerning events as yet unseen, in reverent fear constructed an ark for the saving of his household. By this he condemned the world and became an heir of the righteousness that comes by faith."* (emphasis added).

Both were "justified by faith," to use the New Testament expression and not by any merit of their own.

---

[91] Genesis 5:24

[92] Genesis 6:9

Paul has no difficulty in affirming that "no one is justified before God by the works of the law."

> *"For by works of the law no human being will be justified in his sight, since through the law comes knowledge of sin."*[93]

> *"Yet we know that a person is not justified by works of the law but through faith in Jesus Christ, so we also have believed in Christ Jesus, in order to be justified by faith in Christ and not by works of the law, because by works of the law no one will be justified."* [94]

Listen to Paul's preaching in the synagogue in Antioch Pisidia:

> *"Let it be known to you therefore, brothers, that through this man (Jesus) forgiveness of sins is proclaimed to you, and by him <u>everyone who believes is freed</u> from everything from which <u>you could not be freed by the law of Moses</u>."*[95] (Emphasis added).

If so, then all the Old Testament saints were saved by faith in Christ. And so was Abram.

Paul writes in Ephesians 2:4-9:

> *"But God, being rich in mercy, because of the great love with which he loved us, even when we were dead in our trespasses, made us alive together with*

---

[93] Romans 3:20

[94] Galatians 2:16

[95] Acts 13:38-39

Christ—by grace you have been saved— and raised us up with him and seated us with him in the heavenly places in Christ Jesus, so that in the coming ages he might show the immeasurable riches of his grace in kindness toward us in Christ Jesus. For by grace you have been saved through faith. And this is not your own doing; it is the gift of God, not a result of works, so that no one may boast."

Paul insists in his *magnum opus*, the Epistle to Romans, that Abraham was justified by faith.

"For what does the Scripture say? 'Abraham believed God, and it was counted to him as righteousness.'" [96]

Moreover, since this happened centuries before the Law was given to Moses, he was not justified by keeping the Law, but through faith in God's promises.

John the Baptist scolded Abraham's physical descendants, who were counting on Abraham and his righteousness to please God and escape "from the wrath to come." (Matthew 3:7-10). The religious elite's common claim at the time of John the Baptist and Jesus was that they would have automatic entry into God's presence because they were Abraham's physical descendants. However, John and later, Jesus took them to task and addressed them as "brood of vipers"[97] and "whitewashed sepulchers!" God can raise children for Abraham from stones! What matters is having faith like Abraham that led him to a life of trust and obedience.

---

[96] Romans 4:3

[97] Matthew 3:7; 12:34; 23:27 and 33

Moreover, faith in God must be evidenced by "fruit" in life. We can summarize John the Baptist's teaching in this way: *Abrahamic faith will produce godly behavior, good fruit. If that evidence is not there, none can claim to be Abraham's children!*

> *"But when he saw many of the Pharisees and Sadducees coming to his baptism, he said to them, "You brood of vipers! Who warned you to flee from the wrath to come?* <u>*Bear fruit in keeping with repentance.*</u> *And do not presume to say to yourselves, 'We have Abraham as our father,' for I tell you, God is able from these stones to raise up children for Abraham.''*[98].

John very clearly taught that bearing good fruit is the evidence of having faith. He is demanding that from the physical descendants of Abraham. Merely professing to be the children of Abraham is useless. Give evidence by bearing fruit in keeping up with repentance!

Later Jesus picks up this imagery of "fruit" in His teachings.[99] Paul followed in the footsteps of the Lord and taught the same. Listen to how he summarized this to King Agrippa:

> *"Therefore, O King Agrippa, I was not disobedient to the heavenly vision, but declared first to those in Damascus, then in Jerusalem and throughout all the region of Judea, and also to the Gentiles, that they*

---

[98] Matthew 3:7-9 Emphasis added.

[99] Matthew 7:15-20; 12:33-35. See also Luke 6:43-44

should repent and turn to God, performing deeds in keeping with their repentance."[100]

How crystal clear is the teaching of the Apostle of faith! Genuine faith and repentance will result in the transformation of life and give evidence of that transformation by *"deeds in keeping with repentance."* Here Paul and James say exactly the same thing: *faith without works is dead!*[101] There is no contradiction in the teaching of the Apostles.

Two Imperatives with One *Ultimate* Purpose

"Now the Lord said to Abram, "Go from your country and your kindred and your father's house to the land that I will show you. And I will make of you a great nation, and I will bless you and make your name great, so that you will be a blessing. I will bless those who bless you, and him who dishonors you I will curse, and in you all the families of the earth shall be blessed." Genesis 12:1-3 ESV.[102]

Stephen, in his sermon in Acts 7, tells us that the original call of Abram happened when *"he was in Mesopotamia, before he lived in Haran."* Acts 7:2. Therefore, we know that Genesis 12:1-3 is a retelling of

---

[100] Acts 26:19-20. Emphasis added.

[101] James 2:26.

[102] Christopher J.H. Wright, in his book *The Mission of God*, describes Genesis 12:1-3 as "a pivotal text not only in the book of Genesis but indeed in the whole Bible." Christopher J.H. Wright, *The Mission of God: Unlocking the Bible's Grand Narrative,* (Downers Grove, IL: Intervarsity Press, 2006), p. 194.

Abram's call that happened when he was still living in Ur of the Chaldeans.[103]

The passage that describes the call has two imperatives followed by three result clauses each. So, we can divide it into two parts:

i) First imperative: *"Go."*
    a) I will make you a great nation.
    b) I will bless you.
    c) (I will) make your name great.
ii) *The second imperative: "Be a blessing."*
    a) I will bless those who bless you.
    b) I will curse him who dishonors you.
    c) In you, all the families of the earth shall be blessed.

Therefore, Abram's call was two-fold: a) go to the land that the Lord was going to show him; and b) become a blessing to all the "families of the earth."[104] In other words, it was NEVER just about Abram and his physical descendants alone. *It was always for all the families of the earth, including Abram's physical descendants, as they too are part of "all the families of the earth"!*

---

[103] NIV accurately translates Genesis 12:1: "The LORD **had said** to Abram…." See also the footnote in ESV: *"had said."* Abram's call certainly happened before Genesis 11:31. Then why Genesis 11:31 gives the leadership role for the journey to Terah is a reasonable question. The only logical answer is that the writer expresses due honor to a father.

[104] Apostle Paul describes the promise "in you all the families of the earth shall be blessed" as "gospel in advance" in Galatians 3:6. After noting that, Christopher J.H. Wright states: *"Blessing for the nations is the bottom line, textually and theologically, of God's promise to Abraham."* Wright, *The Mission of God,* p. 194. Author's emphasis.

This is still the purpose of God's call for all. He calls undeserving people, showers them with blessings, transforms them, and makes them instruments of blessings for others. In other words, the purpose for which God calls every single person is a) to bless that person and b) make that person a channel of blessings for others. It is *never* to make that individual a reservoir of blessings!

God repeated the same truth to Abram and his descendants several times, lest they forget this all-important purpose for which He was calling them. We see the promise and purpose always tied together and repeated at critical moments in the patriarchs' lives.

The second time Lord God stated the purpose of Abram's call was after his name was changed from Abram to Abraham. Genesis 18, the first chapter after the story of God changing Abram's name, narrates the history of Abraham and Sarah receiving the promise of the birth of Isaac and Abraham interceding for Sodom.[105]

> *"The Lord said, "Shall I hide from Abraham what I am about to do, seeing that Abraham shall surely become a great and mighty nation, <u>and all the nations of the earth shall be blessed in him</u>?"[106]* Emphasis added.

---

[105] We will deal in detail with the crucial topic of changing the name later. Notably, the name change happens after Abram risks his life to rescue his nephew, who chooses the best land and leaves his uncle with less-than-desirable land. Notice also that it happens 13 years after Ishmael's birth and Hagar's expulsion and return.

[106] Genesis 18:17-19

Then again, at another very crucial chapter in Abraham's life, when he took his only son Isaac to the mountain to sacrifice him in obedience to the Lord's command, the same purpose is repeated.

> *And the angel of the Lord called to Abraham a second time from heaven and said, "By myself I have sworn, declares the Lord, because you have done this and have not withheld your son, your only son, I will surely bless you, and I will surely multiply your offspring as the stars of heaven and as the sand that is on the seashore. And your offspring shall possess the gate of his enemies, and in your offspring[107] shall all the nations of the earth be blessed, because you have obeyed my voice."[108]* Emphasis added.

Lord repeated it to Isaac at a crucial time in his life.

> *And the Lord appeared to him and said, "Do not go down to Egypt; dwell in the land of which I shall tell you. Sojourn in this land, and I will be with you and will bless you, for to you and to your offspring I will give all these lands, and I will establish the oath that I swore to Abraham your father. I will multiply your offspring as the stars of heaven and will give to your offspring all these lands. And in your offspring all the nations of the earth shall be blessed, because Abraham obeyed my voice and*

---

[107] See Galatians 3:16, where Paul identifies the "offspring" in the singular as Christ. "Now the promises were made to Abraham and to his offspring. It does not say, "And to offsprings," referring to many, but referring to one, "And to your offspring," who is Christ."

[108] Genesis 22:15-18

kept my charge, my commandments, my statutes, and my laws."[109] Emphasis added.

Once again, the same purpose is stated to Jacob in the famous dream he had at Bethel.

And he dreamed, and behold, there was a ladder set up on the earth, and the top of it reached to heaven. And behold, the angels of God were ascending and descending on it! And behold, the Lord stood above it and said, "I am the Lord, the God of Abraham your father and the God of Isaac. The land on which you lie I will give to you and to your offspring. Your offspring shall be like the dust of the earth, and you shall spread abroad to the west and to the east and to the north and to the south, <u>and in you and your offspring shall all the families of the earth be blessed</u>."[110] Emphasis added.

God repeating the same promise/purpose is very significant. At the outset of salvation history, God made clear to Abraham's physical descendants that they are a 'chosen' people for a particular purpose: to be an instrument of blessing for all humanity. All of Abraham's physical descendants were to be "a kingdom of priests."[111] for God, not just the tribe of Levi. God's purpose was for ALL of Abraham's children to become "light to the nations,"[112] or "missionaries," if we may use that term. This

---

[109] Genesis 26:2-5

[110] Genesis 28:13-14

[111] Exodus 19:6

[112] Isaiah 42:6

idea is woven all through the history of the people of God in the Old Testament.

Why Did God Change the Name of Abram?

As we already observed, the Holy Bible does not tell us Abram's age when God called him. We know from the sermon of Stephen that Abram was living in Mesopotamia when he received the call.

> *"And Stephen said: 'Brothers and fathers, hear me. The God of glory appeared to our father Abraham when he was in Mesopotamia, before he lived in Haran, and said to him, 'Go out from your land and from your kindred and go into the land that I will show you.' Then he went out from the land of the Chaldeans and lived in Haran. And after his father died, God removed him from there into this land in which you are now living.'"* Acts 7:2-4.

Then he was an idol worshipper (Joshua 24:2). He was sovereignly called and separated from his people to serve the living God. When he was 99 years old, God changed his name from Abram to Abraham (Genesis 17:1-5). What is the significance of this?

The word "name" is found over a thousand times in the Bible. In our world, name is but a label. It was not so in the Biblical world. Name is a reflection of the bearer's character. Along with Abram to Abraham, there are other well-known examples of name-changes in the Bible. Sarai ("My Princess") to Sarah ("Princess")[113], Jacob- "heal catcher," "trickster" or "supplanter."[114]- to Israel[115] and

---

[113] Genesis 17:15.

[114] Genesis 25:26 and 27:36.

Simon to Cephas/Peter[116] are all well-known. As seen in the story of Daniel and the Hebrew boys, we know other cultures also looked upon a person's name as a very important symbol.[117]

When God called him in Ur of the Chaldeans, his name was Abram. Abram means "exalted father." By implication, it could also mean "arrogant or self-centered father." What a great name! Nevertheless, it is a perfect picture of every human being who lives without a personal relationship with the living God.[118] Every single one of us was "Abram" when God called us, totally self-centered and lost in idolatry and sin. Self-centeredness is the worst form of idolatry. Being interested *only* in self is the opposite of loving God and others and laying one's life down for others. Every single one of us, before we were in Christ, was such an idolater.

Name in Hebrew thinking is the reflection of one's character. While it took a while for God to change Abram's name, He changed his name from Abram to *Abraham*. The difference between the two words in Hebrew is only one letter: the fifth letter of the Hebrew alphabet "he" (ה) equivalent to the English letter "h." With that, the meaning of his name, and hence his character, is completely

---

[115] Genesis 32:28 and 35:10.

[116] John 1:42 and Luke 6:14.

[117] Daniel 1:7.

[118] "For he is an example of the vocation of us all; for in him we perceive, that, by the mercy of God, those things which are not are raised from nothing, in order that they may begin to be something." John Calvin, *Calvin's Commentary* on Genesis 12:1.

changed: no longer is he "exalted"; he is now the "father of a multitude of families/peoples or people groups."[119]

It became a common Rabbinic teaching that the fifth letter of the Hebrew alphabet is the symbol of grace. Abram's family practiced idolatry when God called him.[120] God took *Abram*, a self-centered idolater, poured His grace into his life, and transformed him into *Abraham- a source of life and blessing for a multitude of "nations"!* (Genesis 12:3).

Here, we see the purpose for which God calls us. In a way, we are all miniature Abrams! Even today, God calls self-centered idolaters (we all are/were that) and transforms them into sources of blessing for many.

This transformation takes time; *name-change* does not happen all of a sudden. It took God more than twenty-five years to change Abram into Abraham.[121] But

---

[119] The Hebrew word translated "peoples" in NIV and "families" in ESV, KJV, NAS, NRSV, etc., is the equivalent of the NT Greek word "ethna" that is used in the Great Commission. The common English translation is "nations." A far better translation is "people groups" or "ethnic groups." Most Indian languages translate it with the common word "jathi," which is probably one of the best translations. The English concept of "ethnic" comes from the Greek word "ethna" (plural), "ethnos" (singular).

[120] See Joshua 24:2-3.

[121] I say "more than twenty-five years" because we do not know exactly how old Abram was when God first called him. Bible does not tell us his age when the initial encounter took place between Abram and the living God. We know the God of glory appeared to him "while he was still in Mesopotamia before he lived in Haran" (Acts 7:2). The encounter took place in Abram's birthplace, Ur of the Chaldeans (Genesis 15:7 and 11:28).

transformation is mandatory. Abram was an idol worshipper when the living God called him. But he did not remain an idol worshiper; he was transformed into a "friend of God"![122] What a transformation!

The evidence of our call is transformation.

Our *justification* before God happens the moment we believe in Christ, not because of anything we have done, but as a gift because of God's mercy and grace alone, just as Abram's call was not initiated by Abram but by God alone. Paul puts it this way in Romans 3:22-24:[123]

> *"This righteousness is given through faith in Jesus Christ to all who believe. There is no difference between Jew and Gentile, for all have sinned and fall short of the glory of God, and all are justified freely by his grace through the redemption that came by Christ Jesus."*

Paul makes this all-important point more explicit in Ephesians 2: 8-9, where he describes salvation as a gift. *"For it is by grace you have been saved, through faith — and this is not from yourselves, it is the gift of God— not by works, so that no one can boast."*

In Romans 4, when he deals with Abram/Abraham's call, Paul contrasts wages with a gift showing the stark difference between the two. One earns

---

[122] Abram/Abraham is the only person from the Old Testament described as a "friend of God." See 2 Chronicles 20:7, Isaiah 41:8, and James 2:23. Nevertheless, according to John 15:15, every believer in Christ is His friend! What a glorious privilege we have. So, I can boldly declare: "God is my friend"! Hallelujah!

[123] See also Romans 1:17; 10:9-10.

wages and therefore deserves it; one cannot earn a gift. It is based on the grace of the giver. Abram was justified by the grace of God, not because of anything he did. So is every one of us.

Justification by faith is only the beginning of one's walk with God. Just as Abram continued to walk with God and eventually his name was changed to Abraham, we must also walk with God and must be transformed *"to be conformed to the image"* of the Son of God.[124] That's why the New Testament teaches that salvation experience has a *past*, a *present,* and a *future* tense![125]

New Testament uses another powerful imagery to teach this truth: the imagery of birth and growth. When one believes in Jesus (another way of saying "receives the call of God"), he or she is "born again."[126] However, that is only the beginning. The new-born must grow *"to a mature man, to the measure of the stature which belongs to the fullness of Christ."* [127] Peter urges Christians to *"long for the pure spiritual milk that by it you may grow up into salvation."* (2 Peter 2:2). Remaining an infant is being

---

[124] See Romans 8:29.

[125] See Ephesians 2:8 (σεσωσμένοι sesōsmenoi = have been saved), 1 Corinthians 1:18 (σῳζομένοις sōzomenois = are being saved) and Romans 5:9-10 (σωθησόμεθα sōthēsometha =shall be saved). We will talk more about this later.

[126] John 3:3 and 5; 1 Peter 1:23.

[127] Ephesians 4:13. The purpose of the five-fold ministry of the Church is exactly this- maturing of believers. See Ephesians 4: 11ff.

"people of the flesh"[128] and not "spiritual people."[129] (1 Corinthians 3:1).

Another imagery we find in Scripture is that of "walk". In this analogy, when we receive the call of God, when we receive the Lord Jesus Christ as our Savior and Lord, when we are born again, we are beginning a "walk" with Him. *Starting the walk is good, but that is not enough. One must complete it.*[130] Paul repeatedly urges us to "walk worthy" of the call. *"I therefore, a prisoner for the Lord, urge you to walk in a manner worthy of the calling to which you have been called."*[131] The very purpose of baptism is to *"walk in newness of life"*![132]

The theme of the newness of life, new creation, new self, renewal of mind, and renewed spirit is pervasive in all of the Pauline corpus.[133]

---

[128]σάρκινος sarkinos, fleshly, worldly.

[129] πνευματικός pneumatikos, spiritual

[130] "Walk" is not a unique analogy of the New Testament regarding the relationship with God. We already saw that Enoch "walked" with God. See Genesis 5:22 and 24. Again Genesis 6:9 tells us: ".....Noah was a righteous man, blameless in his generation. Noah walked with God." In Malachi 2:6b, God tells about Levi "He walked with me in peace and uprightness, and he turned many from iniquity."

[131] Ephesians 4:1. See also Colossians 1:10, 2:6, and 1 Thessalonians 2:12.

[132] Romans 6:4.

[133] Romans 7:6; 12:2, 2 Corinthians 5:17, Galatians 6:15, Ephesians 4:23,24. Colossians 3:10. The idea of new creation stems directly from the Lord's teaching about new birth to Nicodemus in John 3: 3 and 5.

Paul and John use the picture of "walking in the light" and "walking in darkness" to compare and contrast those who have received the call with those who have not received the call. (John's favorite expression is fellowship with God. One either has fellowship with God, or one does not).

If there is no transformation in us, then we have *not* received the call. Once we hear the call of God and obey, we cannot remain as we are. *"... for at one time you **were** darkness, but now you **are** light in the Lord. Walk as children of light."* Ephesians 5:8.

Walking as children of light is the **evidence** of the call, not the **cause** of the call. We do not **receive** the call because we walk in the light or because of our good behavior. We walk in the light **because** we have received the call. As a result of the call of God, our character reflects the character of God.

Since I started following Christ, has my **name** changed? In other words, is my **character** becoming more like that of Christ? (Romans 8:29) Am I *becoming* Abraham, or am I remaining Abram? This is a critical question that every follower of Christ must answer.

May transformation be the characteristic of our lives! God's purpose in calling us is to make us sources of blessing for others by transforming us from self-centered to other-centered just as our Master Himself became human to serve others and not to be served.[134] *May we fulfill that purpose of our creator!*

---

134 Matthew 20:28; Mark 10:45; 1 Timothy 2:6.

The Key to Being Blessed

Abram's call is the restart of salvation history. We see so many great theological truths in Genesis 12:1-3 which describes this new beginning. An important key to being blessed is found here. The key is in the fifth and sixth promises/blessings and is hidden from many because of a common translation error. Most English translations fail to communicate this critical key for being blessed by translating two completely different Hebrew words using the same English word.[135]

In the fifth promise, God told Abram that if anyone blesses him (Abram), God will bless that person. Here the text uses the common word for blessing in all the Semitic languages- *barakh.*[136]

When we come to the sixth promise, the author of Genesis uses two distinct Hebrew words that most English translations translate with the same word *curse* as NIV: *"and whoever curses you I will curse."* The first word translated as "curse" is the Hebrew word *qalal.*[137] While

---

[135] No translation is perfect. Every translation is an interpretation as it carries the prejudices of the translator(s). Therefore, all of us who have the opportunity must try to acquire at least some basic grasp of the original languages of the Bible. We hope our point here will motivate at least a few readers to learn Biblical Hebrew and Koine Greek.

[136] Many of us remember the first name of the 44th President of the USA, Barack Obama. That name comes from this Semitic word- *barakh* .

[137] קָלַל

qalal in certain contexts can mean "curse"[138] in the context of Genesis 12:3, it is best to translate it as "to treat lightly", "to dishonor," "to look down upon," "to speak ill of," or "to put down,"[139] as it is done in Genesis 16: 4 and 5 where Hagar looks down on Sarai with contempt once she became pregnant.

The second word translated as "curse" in Genesis 12:3 is very different. It is the Hebrew word 'arar,[140] which is used where the Lord curses the serpent for deceiving humanity (Genesis 3:14)[141] and where He curses Cain for murdering his brother (Genesis 4:11). So, it is obvious that 'arar is a far more dire a curse than *qalal*.

Thus, we learn that when anyone blesses Abram, one called by God, God blesses that person. On the other hand, when anyone puts down or looks down upon or treats with contempt, a person who is called by God, God, in turn, "curses" that person.

---

[138] See for example Deuteronomy 23:5 and Joshua 24:9 where *qalal* is used to refer to Balaam's "curse" of the people of God.

[139] ESV has accurately translated the word as "dishonors." NASB has "reviles" in its margin. The new Hindi translation has also rightly translated the word by the English equivalent.

[140] אָרַר

[141] The same word is used by God in 3:17 when He speaks to Adam and tells him that the ground is "cursed" because of his disobedience. It is the word that is also used in 9:25, where Noah curses his son Canaan for exposing his nakedness. See also Genesis 27:29, where Isaac uses the exact words *barakh* and 'arar twice in his blessing of Jacob to say: *"Cursed be those who curse you, And blessed be those who bless you."*

Please carefully note what the Lord promises to Abram. *If anyone "dishonors" Abram or "speaks ill" of him, the Lord Himself will curse (אָרַר 'arar") that person!*

This agrees perfectly with the teaching of our Lord Jesus. In Matthew 5:22b, He taught us: *"....whoever insults his brother will be liable to the council; and whoever says, 'You fool!' will be liable to the hell of fire."*

Paul the Apostle commands us to bless even those who persecute us and not to curse. *"Bless those who persecute you; bless and do not curse them."*[142] The Apostle is simply repeating what our Master taught us: *"bless those who curse you, pray for those who mistreat you."*[143]

Oh! How seriously we need to take every word we utter! May the Lord give me grace to understand this and practice it in my everyday life! I pray the same for you.

---

[142] Romans 12:14.

[143] Luke 6:28.

Chapter 20

The Amazing Love of the Father

The Christian doctrine of salvation is very different from the teachings of all other religions. While all other religions teach that Salvation/Mukti/Moksha/Nirvana[144] is something to be earned by one's efforts, by "karma,"[145] Biblical Christianity declares that salvation is a free gift from God given to those who trust in Him. "By faith alone, by grace alone" is not a slogan; it is the heart of Biblical Christianity.

This central truth of the Gospel comes through vividly in the teachings of our Lord Jesus Christ and His Apostles. We do not have a recorded, explicit statement from the Lord Jesus on this doctrine like the Apostle Paul

---

[144] Mukti/Moksha/Nirvana are words used by Hinduism and Buddhism. For these words, there is no one-to-one correspondence with the Christian doctrine of "salvation" or "eternal life.".

[145] "Karma" is a crucial doctrine both in Hinduism and Buddhism. It has become a common word in English. While the Sanskrit word means "duty" or "action," the doctrine of Karma, stated in straightforward terms, means that one's cumulative actions in previous births determine the current state of life. So, one's goal is to "earn" enough "good karma" to outweigh the effects of "bad karma" and thus achieve a "higher" form of birth and eventually "escape" the "cycle of births and deaths" and become one with the ultimate reality. The sad fact is that even many Christian denominations promulgate some form of "work-righteousness" doctrine. The most notorious example is the teaching of Johann Tetzel (1465-1519). This German Dominican friar promised instant elevation from purgatory to heaven of the dearly departed ones if money were given and indulgences purchased. It is not an isolated teaching of the Catholic Church. Even today, many so-called preachers teach some variation of this vile doctrine, and thousands are deceived.

gives in Ephesians 2: 8 and 9: *For by grace you have been saved through faith. And this is not your own doing; it is the gift of God, nine not a result of works, so that no one may boast."* Yet, we have more than enough of the Lord's teachings in the Gospels to convince us that Apostle Paul and other early Christians learned it from Christ's teaching.

Let's look at one place where the Lord gives us His teaching on soteriology.[146] It is chapter fifteen of Luke's Gospel which is described as the *Gospel in miniature* by many.

Before proceeding further, I must acknowledge my total indebtedness to Dr. Kenneth Bailey for the insights that I have gained on this part of the Scripture. One of the best classes that I had the privilege of "auditing" during my days at Fuller Theological Seminary was a class on Lukan parables taught by Dr. Bailey while he served as Adjunct Professor of New Testament at Fuller during 1975-76. I highly recommend his books to those interested in studying the parables of Jesus from an Eastern perspective. Every single one of his books is worth reading and studying.[147]

---

[146] Soteriology is the branch of theology that studies the doctrine of salvation.

[147] The following are a few books that he has written: *The Cross and the Prodigal: Luke 15 Through the Eyes of Middle Eastern Peasants; The Good Shepherd: A Thousand Year Journey from Psalm 23 to the New Testament; Jesus Through Middle Eastern Eyes- Cultural Studies in the Gospels; Poet and Peasant and Through Peasant Eyes: A Literary-Cultural Approach to the Parables in Luke etc.* If you are getting just one of his books, I highly recommend the last volume, which is a combined volume of two books.

Luke 15 consists of three stories that Jesus told. Of the three stories, the last two are unique to Luke. The last of the three stories, traditionally called the *Parable of the Prodigal Son*,[148], is rightly described as "the most beautiful short story ever told" and "the gospel within the gospel."[149] All the salient elements of the Gospel are in this simple and yet profound story that reveals God's compassionate Father heart.

Matthew reports the first story, that of the one sheep in a hundred *that went astray* and the shepherd who searched for it until he found it and rescued it.[150] (Matthew 18:10-14). Matthew's emphasis in telling the story is on the *preciousness* of each human being, especially little children. He makes that plain by repeating the phrase "little ones" in verses 10 and 14. Note also how Matthew introduces the story in 18:10: *"See that you do not despise one of these little ones. For I tell you that in heaven their angels always see the face of my Father who is in heaven."*

Luke tells the story with a different emphasis. In Luke, the sheep did not stray; the shepherd *lost* it! He then adds two unique stories and combines the three stories as

---

[148] "The Parable of the Prodigal Son" or "The Parable of the Lost Son" is a common title for this story in many English translations. See, for example, ESV and NIV.

[149] *A Tale of Two Sons: The Wastrel and the "Presbyterian": A Parable Revised,* F. Dale Bruner in Christianity Today, October 4, 1985.

[150] It is important to note Matthew and Luke's different emphases in telling the story. While in Matthew, the blame is on the sheep (*"one of them has gone astray"*: the word *astray* is used three times in verses 12 and 13), Luke blames the shepherd ('if he has *lost* one of them" verse 4)! The going astray part gets its full emphasis in Luke's third story.

ONE parable. All three stories must be taken together to understand what the Lord Jesus Christ is teaching us about the central theme of the Scripture: God seeking humanity that has gone astray, that has rebelled and rejected His Fatherly love.

Let's delve into Luke 15. As the first step in understanding Luke 15, it is imperative to note that according to Luke, it is ONE parable in three parts. *"So he told them this parable...."* (Luke 15:3). Please note that Luke uses the single noun *parable* and not the plural *parables* to introduce the following *three stories*.

1. Context of the One Parable with Three Stories:

It is the first rule in rightly interpreting anything: pay close attention to the context! Luke introduces the context of the three stories in the following words:

Luke 15: *1 Now the tax collectors and sinners were all drawing near to hear him. 2 And the Pharisees and the scribes grumbled, saying, "This man receives sinners and eats with them." 3 So he told them this parable:*

The first point to note about the context is that Jesus was *hosting* "tax collectors and sinners" and *eating* with them.

In most cultures hosting and eating with one another is a sign of fully accepting the other. This is true even today. We can only imagine how strong such attitudes were two thousand years ago.

Let me narrate my own experience. When growing up as a child in India, I had a very good buddy who worked on my father's farm. Though much older than I, he was my best friend. He would pretend to be an elephant and let me ride on his back and play with me whenever he could.

When meal times came, I would compel him to sit with me and eat. But, to my utter bewilderment and disappointment, he refused to sit with me and eat. He would take his dish and go to a corner and sit there and eat alone! I remember crying and asking him to sit with me. But he refused. I thought he didn't really like me and that's why he didn't sit with me. Only when I grew up did I realize the real reason. Our society was steeped in "caste" differences and my best friend was told by the society that he was not good enough to sit with me and eat. Because only "equals" were permitted to sit together and eat, and he was not my "equal" in our social structure!

Such attitude was stronger among the people of the Middle East during the time of Jesus. In the words of Kenneth Bailey, even today: "To eat with another person in the Mideast *is a sacramental act* signifying acceptance in a very deep level."[151] As Bailey observes, a generous wealthy person might feed a lot of poor people. *But he will not eat with them.*[152] Eating with another was (and is) the most intimate relationship one could enter into with another outside of marriage!

Bailey quotes the eminent New Testament scholar Joachim Jeremias who wrote:

> *"To understand what Jesus was doing in eating with "sinners," it is important to realize that in the east, even today, to invite a man to a meal was an honour. It was an offer of peace, trust, brotherhood and forgiveness; in short, sharing a table meant*

---

[151] Kenneth E. Bailey, The Cross & the Prodigal, p. 29. Emphasis added.

[152] Kenneth E. Bailey, *Poet & Peasant AND Through Peasant Eyes, p. 143.*

206

sharing life...Thus Jesus' meals with publicans and sinners...are an expression of the mission and message of Jesus (Mark 2:17),... The inclusion of sinners in the community of salvation, achieved in table-fellowship, is the most meaningful expression of the message of the redeeming love of God."[153]

We must understand the invitation given in Revelation 3:20 in light of this deeply held cultural attitude:

"Behold, I stand at the door and knock. If anyone hears my voice and opens the door, I will come in to him and eat with him, and he with me." The invitation is to enter into the most intimate fellowship with Christ: *"I will...eat with him, and he with me."*

We know that the issue was alive and well in the early Church. The conflict between Paul and Peter described in Galatians 2:11-12 was centered on this issue.

Please take special note of the wording that the Pharisees and scribes use: *"This man receives...."*[154] The word translated receive (*prosdechomai)* is a stronger form of the common word *dechomai* ("to receive") and means *"to welcome into fellowship."* [155] Obviously, Jesus is the host of this event. In the eyes of the religious elite, Jesus was defiling himself by receiving and eating with "tax collectors and sinners."

---

[153] Joachim Jeremias, Theology, p 115f. quoted by Bailey, Poet & Peasant...., p142-43.

[154] See also Mark 2:15ff.

[155] Kenneth Bailey, *The Cross & the Prodigal*, p. 28.

Jesus was known as a "friend of tax collectors and sinners."[156] He chose Levi, also known as Matthew, a tax collector, to be one of his Apostles![157]

In the eyes of Jesus, tax collectors, and sinners were far closer to the Kingdom than the religious elites such as Pharisees and scribes.[158] He had a very low opinion of those who were religious externally and, at the same, were far away from God in their hearts. The parable of the Pharisee and the tax collector praying (Luke 18:10-13) clearly illustrates that.

Pharisees and scribes, on the other hand, despised Jesus and constantly criticized him for associating with such people. In their eyes, tax collectors and sinners were not good enough to enter the Kingdom of God and were rejected by God even though they were Abraham's physical descendants.

Tax collectors were Jewish people like Levi (Matthew), though Israelites, who had sided with the occupying Romans, and therefore considered as traitors by most Jews. They were excluded from all social contacts by pious Jews and were not allowed to enter a synagogue or the Temple. The reason that the tax collector in the parable of Jesus had to "stand far off" (Luke 18:13) when he prayed was because of this restriction.

---

[156] Matthew 11:19; Luke 7:34.

[157] Luke 5:27; Matthew 10:3.

[158] Matthew 21:31

Who were "sinners"? They, too, were physical descendants of Abraham. But because of their inability to keep all the rigorous laws of cleanliness and purification, they were rejected as "people of the land" (*'am ha-'arets*)[159] and deemed "unclean." Pharisees refused to eat with them and accept them as equals.

For example, shepherds were considered "sinners' by Pharisees. Reasons?

    a) As they were constant companions to sheep, they could not keep all the "traditions of the elders" regarding cleanliness and washing of hands and feet.[160] They also smelled like sheep. According to the religious elites of Jesus' time, such people were not acceptable to God.

    b) Moreover, they could not live up to the strict interpretation of Exodus 22:5, which states: *"If a man causes a field or vineyard to be grazed over, or lets his beast loose and it feeds in another man's field, he shall make restitution from the best in his own field and in his own vineyard."* While shepherds guided their sheep into pastures, no matter how careful they were not to encroach into other people's land, their animals often strayed into other peoples' property. It was humanly impossible to keep track of all such violations and compensate the parties concerned. Therefore, in the eyes of the very strict legalistic religious leaders, all shepherds became de facto "sinners"!

---

[159] Kenneth E. Bailey, *Finding the Lost: Cultural Keys to Luke 15,* p.59.

[160] Mark 7:3-4.

Bailey reports that the list of proscribed trades for a Jew is listed in Mishna and Talmud[161], and herdsmen are mentioned twice as a trade that is not fitting for a righteous person. A few of the other trades mentioned are innkeepers, tanners, physicians, camel and ass drivers, and sailors![162]

The sense of humor of God in dealing with self-righteous people who condemned others on the basis of what they did to make a living can clearly be seen right at the beginning of the Gospel story. [163]

Who received the revelation of the birth of the Messiah first? Not the religious elite in Jerusalem, but humble shepherds, the rejected ones, who were watching over their sheep in the open (Luke 2:8ff). Note that only Luke, the Gentile Gospel writer, tells this story!

In Matthew's Gospel, the revelation comes to the Magi, the Wise Men from the East. Who are these? These are Gentiles, despised in the eyes of the self-righteous and called "dogs" by them! Is it not shocking and surprising that none of the religious leaders in Jerusalem received the revelation of the birth of the Messiah?

Not only did they not receive the revelation from God while despised shepherds and Gentiles did receive it, they did not believe the testimony of those who received

---

[161] Kenneth E. Bailey, *Finding the Lost: Cultural Keys to Luke* 15, p.65

[162] Joachim Jeremias, *Jerusalem in the Time of Jesus* (Philadelphia: Fortress, 1969), p.304.

[163] The terrible caste system in India, which is still very strong in most of the country, is based on two external characteristics of people: the color of their skin (*Varnasram)* and the nature of their occupation (*Karmasram*).

the revelation. Look at their response to the testimony of the Magi, who travelled hundreds of miles, facing all kinds of dangers, following the star. When Herod assembled *"all the people's chief priests and teachers of the law"* and asked them *"where the Messiah was to be born,"* they answered instantly, *"In Bethlehem in Judea,"* and quoted Micah 5:2.[164]

Yet, did any of them go with the Magi to see the Messiah? Not one!

The despised shepherds went to the manger and saw the Word that became flesh.

> *"When the angels went away from them into heaven, the shepherds said to one another, "Let us go over to Bethlehem and see this thing that has happened, which the Lord has made known to us." And they went with haste and found Mary and Joseph, and the baby lying in a manger.* (Luke 2:15-16 ESV).

Magi went and worshipped the one "born the king of the Jews.

> *"And going into the house, they saw the child with Mary his mother, and they fell down and worshiped him. Then, opening their treasures, they offered him gifts, gold and frankincense and myrrh."* (Matthew 2:2, 11).

---

[164] Matthew 2:1ff., especially verses 2-6. Note also verse 9ff: "After they heard the king, they went on their way.." Also, note the repeated use of "they" by Matthew. Matthew uses the word "they" seven times (NIV and ESV). Is it to emphasize that none of the "chief priests and the teachers of the law" accompanied them?

But none of the learned chief priests and the teachers of the law bothered to go to Bethlehem and check out what the Magi said. Was their faith merely theoretical? They knew and yet did not know. May the Lord help us not to have such faith! *What we believe must lead to action, to obedience. Otherwise, we are foolish builders who are building our foundation on sand, and all that we build will collapse sooner or later.*[165]

Jesus choosing one of the despised tax collectors to be his Apostle is another amazing declaration that he came not to seek the righteous but sinners. Then he chose a gentile physician as one of the Gospel writers!

So, we need to understand the expression "sinners" as including ordinary people, "people of the land" (*'am ha-'arets*), such as shepherds, tanners, camel drivers, sailors etc., who did not qualify as "the righteous" in the eyes of the religious leaders and thus rejected by them. Jesus *received them and ate with them*. This infuriated the Pharisees and scribes and they *grumbled* against him (Luke 15:1-2). The word translated grumbled/muttered/murmured is the same word used in the Septuagint (LXX)[166] for the repeated murmuring of the people against Moses as he was leading them out of Egypt.[167]

It is very important to note that the remainder of Luke 15 is Lord Jesus' response to this murmuring. It is directly addressed to the ones who were criticizing him.

---

[165] Matthew 7:24-27.

[166] Septuagint (LXX) is the Greek translation of the Old Testament from the original Hebrew, believed to have been made for the Jewish community in Egypt in the 3rd and 2nd century BC.

[167] Bailey, *The Cross & the Prodigal,* p. 28.

Note 15:3: *So he told them this parable...* If we miss this point, we will fail to understand what Jesus is teaching through the three stories that follow.

2. "From the light to the heavy"- Jesus, the masterful Rabbi.

Before we look into the parable itself, let's learn about a common Rabbinic teaching method. Rabbis commonly used a teaching technique that is known as the *qal wahomer*, meaning "from the light to the heavy." It is attributed to the famous Rabbi Hillel, who died around 10 A.D. In this method of teaching, one begins with the simple and easy and proceeds to the complex and difficult. The three stories in Luke 15 are perfect examples of *qal wahomer*.

In the first story, a shepherd who has one hundred sheep loses one of them. Loss is one percent. In the second story, a woman who has ten coins loses one. Loss is ten percent. In the final story, there are two sons. How many are lost? If you answered "one" as most Christians normally do, then you must read the rest of this very carefully! Both are lost! See the steady progress: one percent, ten percent, and finally, one hundred percent. Jesus affirms the foundational Biblical doctrine of the "fall" of humanity from the way God created them to the current state of depravity summarized by Paul in Romans 3:23: *"All have sinned and come short of the glory of God."*

Remember, Jesus is telling these stories to the Pharisees and scribes in response to their fierce criticism that he is eating with people who are not good enough for God. Pharisees claimed that they were perfect people and that God was interested only in people who were perfect like them.168 Jesus demolishes their argument through these amazingly simple yet profound stories. When we come to the final of the three stories, we see them clearly pictured in the older son who thought like them that he has "never disobeyed your command. . ." (15:29b) and yet had no relationship with his father or his brother and thought of himself as a "slave." (See 15:29a).

3. **First story: The Shepherd who seeks the one lost sheep: Luke 15:4-7.**

> *"What man of you, having a hundred sheep, if he has lost one of them, does not leave the ninety-nine in the open country, and go after the one that is lost, until he finds it? ⁵ And when he has found it, he lays it on his shoulders, rejoicing. ⁶ And when he comes home, he calls together his friends and his neighbors, saying to them, 'Rejoice with me, for I have found my sheep that was lost.' ⁷ Just so, I tell you, there will be more joy in heaven over one sinner who repents than over ninety-nine righteous persons who need no repentance.* (ESV).

Note how Jesus opens the story bearing in mind what we just learned. The religious elite looked down upon a shepherd as impure and not worthy to enter the presence of God. But look how Jesus addresses such people! The sense of humor and courage of the Lord come through right away. He calls them shepherds: *"What man of you, having a hundred sheep!"*

---

168 Listen to the prayer of the Pharisee in the Parable of the Pharisee and Tax Collector: *"The Pharisee, standing by himself, prayed thus: 'God, I thank you that I am not like other men, extortioners, unjust, adulterers, or even like this tax collector. ¹² I fast twice a week; I give tithes of all that I get."* Luke 18:11-12.

The common people who heard must have burst into laughter as Jesus said these words![169]

".... if he has lost one of them..."

Not only does Jesus address his adversaries as "shepherds," he puts the responsibility of "losing the sheep," such as tax collectors, tanners, inn-keepers, camel drivers, shepherds, etc. (in short, the "people of the land") squarely on their shoulders just as Jeremiah and Ezekiel did centuries ago![170]

Kenneth Bailey tells us:

"The very structure of life and language in the Middle East requires that people do not blame themselves. No one says, "I lost my sheep." The appropriate idiom is "the sheep went from me." I did not "miss the train" but rather "the train left me."[171]

---

[169] As Bailey points out, it is a real puzzle how shepherds became "unclean" by the time of Jesus when we find Yahweh himself pictured as the shepherd (Psalm 23:1), and David and Moses are pictured as shepherds. See Bailey, *Finding the Lost, p. 65; Poet and Peasant and Through Peasant Eyes,* p. 147. After stating that herdsmen appear in the rabbinic lists of proscribed trades, Bailey quotes Joachim Jeremias as follows: ". . . most of the times they (shepherds) were dishonest and thieving; they led their herds on to other people's land. . . . and pilfered the produce of the herd." Quoted from Jeremias, *Jerusalem in the Time of Jesus,* p. 305 and 310f.

[170] See below.

[171] Bailey, *Finding the Lost,* p. 65

He also points out that the story in Matthew does put the blame on the sheep: *"if.... one of them has gone astray..."* (Matthew 18:12).

But here in Luke, it is the shepherd who lost the sheep. This is a direct attack on the leaders of Israel. It is because of their failure the sheep ("the people of the land- *'am ha-'arets ?*), is lost. Jesus is recalling the famous passages from Jeremiah 50: 6ff and Ezekiel 34:1ff where the great prophets of the Old Testament condemned the leaders of Israel in very harsh terms.

Jeremiah 50:6

> *"My people have been lost sheep. Their shepherds have led them astray, turning them away on the mountains. From mountain to hill they have gone. They have forgotten their fold."*

Ezekiel 34:1-10

> *"The word of the LORD came to me:* [2] *"Son of man, prophesy against the shepherds of Israel; prophesy, and say to them, even to the shepherds, Thus says the Lord GOD: Ah, shepherds of Israel who have been feeding yourselves! Should not shepherds feed the sheep?* [3] *You eat the fat, you clothe yourselves with the wool, you slaughter the fat ones, but you do not feed the sheep.* [4] *The weak you have not strengthened, the sick you have not healed, the injured you have not bound up, the strayed you have not brought back, the lost you have not sought, and with force and harshness you have ruled them.* [5] *So they were scattered, because there was no shepherd, and they became food for all the wild beasts. My sheep were scattered;* [6] *they wandered over all the mountains and on every high hill. My*

sheep were scattered over all the face of the earth, with none to search or seek for them.

[7] "Therefore, you shepherds, hear the word of the LORD: [8]As I live, declares the Lord GOD, surely because my sheep have become a prey, and my sheep have become food for all the wild beasts, since there was no shepherd, and because my shepherds have not searched for my sheep, but the shepherds have fed themselves, and have not fed my sheep, [9] therefore, you shepherds, hear the word of the LORD: [10] Thus says the Lord GOD, Behold, I am against the shepherds, and I will require my sheep at their hand and put a stop to their feeding the sheep. No longer shall the shepherds feed themselves. I will rescue my sheep from their mouths, that they may not be food for them."

By recalling these famous Messianic passages from the great prophets Jeremiah and Ezekiel, Jesus is directly claiming that he is the Shepherd who has come to search for the lost sheep of God. He is the fulfillment of Ezekiel's prophecy:

Ezekiel 34:11-16:

"For thus says the Lord GOD: Behold, I, I myself will search for my sheep and will seek them out. [12] As a shepherd seeks out his flock when he is among his sheep that have been scattered, so will I seek out my sheep, and I will rescue them from all places where they have been scattered on a day of clouds and thick darkness. [13] And I will bring them out from the peoples and gather them from the countries, and will bring them into their own land. And I will feed them on the mountains of Israel, by the ravines, and in all the inhabited places of the

country. [14] I will feed them with good pasture, and on the mountain heights of Israel shall be their grazing land. There they shall lie down in good grazing land, and on rich pasture they shall feed on the mountains of Israel. [15] I myself will be the shepherd of my sheep, and I myself will make them lie down, declares the Lord GOD. [16] I will seek the lost, and I will bring back the strayed, and I will bind up the injured, and I will strengthen the weak, and the fat and the strong I will destroy.[1] I will feed them in justice."

While the religious leaders of Israel rejected most of the common people as "unclean" and unworthy of God, Jesus mingled with them, sought them, taught them, and ate with them.

"...does not leave the ninety-nine in the open country, and go after the one that is lost, until he finds it? [5] And when he has found it, he lays it on his shoulders, rejoicing."

Every sheep is precious to a good shepherd. While a hireling does not care for them and would flee when a wolf attacks them, a good shepherd will lay his life down for the sheep. (John 10:10-13).

The image of a shepherd carrying a sheep on his shoulders is a familiar picture for us. While we might look upon such a picture as beautiful, cute, or even romantic, the fact of the matter is that restoring a lost sheep to its fold was painful, hard work.

We are told that the early Eastern images of the Good Shepherd carrying the lost sheep over his shoulders showed a very large sheep and a rather frail, small shepherd to communicate the difficulties in searching, finding, and

218

restoring a lost sheep.[172] The shepherd had to pay a price in order to find and rescue the lost. "A lost sheep will lie down helplessly and refuse to budge. The shepherd is forced to carry it over long distances."[173] As Norval Geldenhuys has written: "...the shepherd considers no trouble, sacrifice and suffering too great to find the lost sheep and bring it back."[174] Our text says: *And when he has found it, he lays it on his shoulders, rejoicing.*" The shepherd *rejoices* in the burden of carrying the found sheep. This statement of Jesus is an open rebuke to the angry Pharisees and scribes who were muttering and murmuring instead of rejoicing with Jesus as he is rescuing the "lost sheep" of Israel.

A very important point to note is that this joy in carrying a heavy sheep is the foreshadowing of the suffering of Christ on the Cross to "find" us who were lost. It becomes clearer as we come to the final story.

It is often asked: "What happened to the ninety-nine sheep? Does not the story tell that the shepherd left the ninety-nine in the wilderness? How can a caring shepherd do that to the ninety-nine sheep?" Here we have to remember another important principle in interpreting any parable. We must remember that it is a parable, to begin with.[175] All the details are not be pressed in interpreting a

---

[172] Bailey, *Finding the Lost*, p. 76.

[173] Bailey, *Poet & Peasant,* p. 148.

[174] Norval Geldenhuys, *Commentary on the Gospel of Luke,* The New International Commentary on the New Testament, Eerdmans Publishing Co., *Grand R*apids, MI. 1951. P. 402.

[175] The word parable comes from the Greek word "parabole," which means comparison, illustration, or analogy. "Parabole" is made up of

parable. It is obvious that a shepherd who cares for one lost sheep will never endanger the ninety-nine and make provision to care for them while he goes out to search for the one that is lost. Moreover, the joyous note at the end of the story assures us that all one hundred are safe. Otherwise, how can there be such great joy for the shepherd?

Another question that naturally arises from the concluding sentence of the story:

> *"Just so, I tell you, there will be more joy in heaven over one sinner who repents than over ninety-nine righteous persons who need no repentance."* (verse 7).

The question is: "Are there righteous persons who have no need to repent?"

A group of Rabbis during the time of Jesus did teach that there are people who are "perfectly righteous" and do not need to repent. Bailey quotes from the Talmud to show that such a view did exist.[176] Some Rabbis taught that Abraham, Isaac, and Jacob were sinless.[177]

But such a view is contrary to the Old Testament texts such as 1 Kings 8:46 "…there is no man who does not

---

two Greek words, "para," meaning "to come alongside" or "compare" + "ballo," meaning 'to throw" or "see with."

[176] Bailey, *Poet & Peasant,* p. 154. Also see, *Finding the Lost,* p. 88-89. One has to wonder whether Apostle Paul's words in Philippians 3:6 that "touching the righteousness which is in the law" he was "blameless" is a reflection of such a view he held during his pre-Christian days.

[177] Bailey, *Finding the Lost,* p. 88-89.

sin...," and Isaiah 53:6: *All of us like sheep have gone astray, Each of us has turned to his own way;"*

Therefore, Jesus must be using the phrase here as an irony as we know the Holy Bible does teach that all need to repent: *"All have sinned and come short of the glory of God"* is the loud declaration of both Old Testament and New Testament.[178]

Another key insight from the first story is a new understanding of repentance. Pharisees taught that repentance is a prerequisite to receiving grace.[179] They taught that repentance is primarily a human action. Bailey's quotation of George F. More is very helpful in understanding the Rabbinic teaching on repentance.

> *"To the Jewish definition of repentance belong the reparation of injuries done to a fellow man in his person, property, or good name, the confession of sin, prayer for forgiveness, and the genuine resolve and endeavor not to fall into the sin again."[180]*

Bailey identifies three elements of repentance as Rabbis taught:

1. "Compensation offered;
2. Confession made;
3. Resolve/endeavor not to sin again."[181]

---

[178] Psalm 14:1-3; Psalm 53:1-3; Romans 3:23.

[179] Bailey, *Poet & Peasant*, p. 155. See also *Finding the Lost,* p. 86 to 88.

[180] Bailey, *Finding the Lost,* p. 87.

[181] Bailey, *Finding the Lost,* p. 87.

Bailey continues: *"The idea that repentance is a "work" which man does prior to God's acceptance of him is found all through rabbinic literature."*[182]

The story of the lost and found sheep teaches that repentance is "being found." The sheep did not do anything to be found other than it got lost! So, a radically new understanding of repentance is introduced by Jesus. This is developed further as we proceed to the second and third stories.

When we come to the third story, "being found" alone becomes insufficient for entering into a relationship with the Father. We can say that the older son was, in a way, "found," and yet he refused to go into the Father's house! So, there is more to repentance than just being "found." Wait and see as we pursue the story further!

Joy is the predominant theme that rings out at the close of the story. The words "rejoice," and "joy" are repeated three times in this short story. Jesus is contrasting the murmuring and unhappy attitude of the Pharisees and scribes with the joy in the presence of God concerning even one child of God who returns to Him.

4. The Second Story: The Woman Who Lost and Found the Coin.

> Luke 15:8-10 *"Or what woman, having ten silver coins, if she loses one coin, does not light a lamp and sweep the house and seek diligently until she finds it? [9] And when she has found it, she calls together her friends and neighbors, saying, 'Rejoice with me, for I have found the coin that I had lost.' [10]*

---

[182] Bailey, *Poet & Peasant,* p. 179.

Just so, I tell you, there is joy before the angels of God over one sinner who repents."

While the first story begins with the phrase *"What man of you,"* the second story begins with *"Or what woman,"* omitting for obvious reasons the words "of you," as the Lord's audience was, most likely, exclusively men.

In the first story, Jesus uses the "unclean" shepherd as his hero. In the second story, the place is taken by a despised woman. Listen to Bailey:

> *"In the cultural world of first-century Palestine, the very use of a woman in an illustration required a moral decision. Jesus is again rejecting Pharisaic attitudes toward groups of people in society. First, it was the proscribed shepherds, now the inferior woman."[183]*

The second story is very similar to the first in many respects. At the same time, there are differences as well. It is an inanimate coin that is lost in the second story. As most women in the time of Jesus were confined to their houses most of the time, the woman who lost the coin is sure that she lost it in the house, and so does everything she can to find it. While the effort to find the lost coin is not as burdensome as finding a lost sheep, nonetheless, she spares no effort to find it. She lights a lamp, sweeps the whole house "and seeks diligently until she finds it."

A coin was very precious to an ordinary person. Some scholars believe it was probably part of her dowry that she proudly wore around her neck. William Barclay

---

[183] Bailey, *Poet & Peasant,* p. 158. He points out that if the word "woman" was to be used in conversation among men, an apology was required in conservative areas!

thinks that the coin was a part of the headdress made of ten silver coins linked together by a silver chain worn as the mark of a married woman.[184] Losing that is not only a financial loss; it is also shameful. Jesus' society was a shame and honor-based society.

Both stories end with the dominant theme of joy. While the shepherd invites only his male friends, the woman invites only her female friends, a cultural detail lost in English translations but apparent in the original text.

Jesus contrasts the grumbling and angry attitude of the Pharisees with the joy in the presence of God, even when one straying human comes home. Pharisees ought to be rejoicing that their fellow brothers and sisters are being sought and brought home by Jesus. Instead, they were angry and upset with Jesus.

5. **The Final Story: The Two Lost Sons. (A far better title might be "The Incredible Love of the Father." A love so strong that it compels him to suffer humiliation to "find" his lost sons.)**[185]

> Luke 15: 11-32. *[11]And He said, "A man had two sons. [12] "The younger of them said to his father, 'Father, give me the share of the estate that falls to me.' So he divided his wealth between them.[13] "And not many days later, the younger son gathered*

---

[184] William Barclay, *The Gospel of Luke, Revised Edition,* The Westminster Press, Philadelphia, PA. 1975. P.202.

[185] William Barclay argues that the story "should never have been called the parable of the Prodigal Son, for the son is not the hero. It should be called the parable of the Loving Father, for it tells us rather about a father's love than a son's sin." William Barclay, *The Gospel of Luke,* p. 205.

everything together and went on a journey into a distant country, and there he squandered his estate with loose living. ¹⁴ *"Now when he had spent everything, a severe famine occurred in that country, and he began to be impoverished.* ¹⁵ *"So he went and hired himself out to one of the citizens of that country, and he sent him into his fields to feed swine.* ¹⁶ *"And he would have gladly filled his stomach with the pods that the swine were eating, and no one was giving anything to him.* ¹⁷ *"But when he came to ¹his senses, he said, 'How many of my father's hired men have more than enough bread, but I am dying here with hunger!* ¹⁸ *'I will get up and go to my father, and will say to him, "Father, I have sinned against heaven, and in your sight;* ¹⁹ *I am no longer worthy to be called your son; make me as one of your hired men."'* ²⁰ *"So he got up and came to his father. But while he was still a long way off, his father saw him and felt compassion for him, and ran and embraced him and kissed him.* ²¹ *"And the son said to him, 'Father, I have sinned against heaven and in your sight; I am no longer worthy to be called your son.'* ²² *"But the father said to his slaves, 'Quickly bring out the best robe and put it on him, and put a ring on his hand and sandals on his feet;* ²³ *and bring the fattened calf, kill it, and let us eat and celebrate;* ²⁴ *for this son of mine was dead and has come to life again; he was lost and has been found.' And they began to celebrate.*

²⁵ *"Now his older son was in the field, and when he came and approached the house, he heard music and dancing.* ²⁶ *"And he summoned one of the servants and began inquiring what these things could be.* ²⁷ *"And he said to him, 'Your brother has come, and your father has killed the fattened calf*

because he has received him back safe and sound.'
²⁸ "But he became angry and was not willing to go in; and his father came out and began pleading with him. ²⁹ "But he answered and said to his father, 'Look! For so many years I have been serving you and I have never neglected a command of yours; and yet you have never given me a young goat, so that I might celebrate with my friends; ³⁰ but when this son of yours came, who has devoured your wealth with prostitutes, you killed the fattened calf for him.' ³¹ "And he said to him, 'Son, you have always been with me, and all that is mine is yours. ³² 'But we had to celebrate and rejoice, for this brother of yours was dead and has begun to live, and was lost and has been found.'"[186]

Remember, these three stories form ONE PARABLE, according to Luke. That is crucial to remember to understand what the Scripture is teaching.

The final story has two parts, which is obvious to any reader. Part one primarily deals with the younger son and part two with the older son. Let's look at the story in depth.

Part One: The Younger Son.

Opening Scene: At Home.

"And He said, "A man had two sons. ¹² "The younger of them said to his father, 'Father, give me

---

[186] Often called "the greatest short story in the world." See William Barclay, *The Gospel of Luke*, p. 204. Also known as "the Gospel within the Gospel." Norval Geldenhuys, *Commentary on the Gospel of Luke*, p. 406.

the share of the estate that falls to me.' So he divided his wealth between them." Luke 15:11-12.

There are several jarring features right here in the opening of the story. But, as we are far removed from the cultural milieu of Jesus and his audience, we read these words and pass on as if nothing significant happens here. When the audience of Jesus heard these words, they all gasped because such a thing was unheard of in their society. They instantly understood that what the younger son said in effect was:

"Father, I wish you were dead so I can have my inheritance to do what I really want to do with it." [187]

Listen to Bailey's words:

"... the startling fact is that, to my knowledge, in all of Middle Eastern literature (aside from this parable) from ancient times to the present, there is no case of any son, older or younger, asking for his inheritance from a father who is still in good health." [188]

The appropriate reaction of the father ought to have been according to Deuteronomy 21:18-21: stone him to death![189] A typical Eastern father would have become

---

[187] Bailey, *Finding the Lost,* p. 112-114; *Poet & Peasant,* p. 161-169; *The Cross and the Prodigal*, p. 38-41.

[188] Bailey, *Poet & Peasant*, p. 164.

[189] Deut. 21:18 "If a man has a stubborn and rebellious son who will not obey the voice of his father or the voice of his mother, and, though they discipline him, will not listen to them, [19] then his father and his mother shall take hold of him and bring him out to the elders of his city at the gate of the place where he lives, [20] and they shall say

furious and, at the least, drove the son out of his home. But to the utter shock of Jesus' audience, this father did what was least expected of him: *"So he divided his wealth between them."*

Because of our cultural ignorance, we miss another crucial point of the story. Notice that Jesus opened the story by saying, *"A man had two sons"* and *"he divided his wealth between them."* It is the *younger* son who makes the shocking request. People who heard Jesus will instinctively ask:

> *"Where is the older boy? Why is he not intervening? Why did he accept his share?"*

In the order of priority, after the father comes the older son. If there is any conflict between the father and anyone else, particularly between the father and the younger son, it was the duty of the older son to intervene and bring reconciliation. The first question that would rise in the mind of everyone who listened to Jesus is why was the older son not doing his duty.

Secondly, he was expected to refuse the transfer of property to him as that was to be done only after the father's death. Through his silence and inaction, the older son was declaring to the world that all was not well between him, his father, and his younger brother![190]

---

to the elders of his city, 'This our son is stubborn and rebellious; he will not obey our voice; he is a glutton and a drunkard.' [21] Then all the men of the city shall stone him to death with stones. So you shall purge the evil from your midst, and all Israel shall hear, and fear.

[190] Bailey, *The Cross & the Prodigal*, p. 44-46. See also *Poet & the Peasant,* p. 168. One has to wonder whether the younger son wants to run away because of this broken relationship with his brother.

When Jesus' audience heard the words: *"So he divided his wealth between them,"* they must have been shocked again as no father in the Middle East of the time of Jesus would do that. It is also important to note the Greek word translated as *"his wealth"* by ESV. King James uses the phrase "his living" to translate the original word "bios" from which we get the word biology in English. Bailey points out Arabic, Coptic, and Aramaic translations that translate the word as *"life."*[191] Is Jesus picturing more than a human father? Is he talking about the very gift of life to us? Yes, for sure.

Father's action of graciously giving away his wealth even to a blatantly rebellious son demonstrates that this father is very different from any other father. Even though in the story there is no strict one-to-one correspondence for the father with God, in this father, we are beginning to have a glimpse of a heavenly father whose love is beyond anything human, who *"causes his sun to rise on the evil and the good, and sends rain on the righteous and the unrighteous."*[192] This father's love is so great that he gives freedom to reject his love. Let us not forget that when someone loves someone deeply and that someone rejects that love, it is excruciatingly painful. Father's heart is indeed deeply wounded by the rejection of his love by the younger son at the story's opening, and when we come to

---

Remember Jacob and Esau? See Kenneth E. Bailey, *Jacob & the Prodigal,* Downers Grove, IL: InterVarsity Press, 2003.

[191] Bailey, *Finding the Lost,* p. 119.

[192] Matthew 5:45.

the end of the story, we see the same rejection by the older son, too![193]

Scene #2: "Far County."

> *"And not many days later, the younger son gathered everything together and went on a journey into a distant country, and there he squandered his estate with loose living."* Luke 15:13.

The younger son was not happy just to receive his share of the estate. He wanted a complete break with his father and brother. So, he does that which is unthinkable in the context of the community of Jesus. He quickly disposes off his ancestral property! Under exceptional circumstances, a father might give shares of his property to his children while he was living. Even then, they were not permitted to sell the property. Only after the father's death was such a sale permitted.[194]

But this father is so very different that he not only gives his property to the son, he allows him to sell it! This again demonstrates the amazing love of the father. Ancestral property was extremely precious, and a person would rather die than sell it, as seen in Naboth's story. His words to Ahab, *"The LORD forbid that I should give you the inheritance of my fathers."* (2 Kings 21:3) illustrate this attachment.

We must know another cultural fact to understand the seriousness of the younger son's actions. He cut off his relationship with the community by disposing of the ancestral property. If a Jew lost his property to a Gentile,

---

[193] Jesus crying for Jerusalem is a poignant picture of this love

[194] Bailey, *Poet & the Peasant,* p. 163.

the community would hold a ceremony that was known as *qesasah (or Kezazah)*, which means *"a cutting off."*[195] They would break a large earthenware vessel filled with various nuts and burned corn and shout: *"So and so is cut off from his people."* Once that is done, he will not be admitted back to the community. Thus, his journey to "a far country" is a total break from his father and brother and the community that nourished him.

Scene #3: In a Pig Pen

> [14] *"Now when he had spent everything, a severe famine occurred in that country, and he began to be impoverished.* [15] *"So he went and hired himself out to one of the citizens of that country, and he sent him into his fields to feed swine.* [16] *"And he would have gladly filled his stomach with the pods that the swine were eating, and no one was giving anything to him."* Luke 15:14-16.

We will not dwell too long on this scene as it is familiar to most of us. He quickly wasted his father's riches and became a pauper. All his friends left him and he was in utter need. Yet, his pride and sense of shame did not allow him to return to his father. Instead, he tried his best to find ways to fill his stomach by working for others.

The phrase "hired himself out" is translated from the original text, which says "he glued himself" to the man.[196] Anyone who has traveled to India, for example,

---

[195] Bailey, *Poet & Peasant,* p. 167; *The Cross & the Prodigal,* p. 52-53; *Finding the Lost,* p. 121-122.

[196] Bailey, *Poet & Peasant,* p. 170; *Finding the Lost,* p. 126; *The Cross & the Prodigal,* p. 56. The Greek word *kollaö,* translated as "hired himself out" by ESV, comes from the word for glue, "kola."

will know precisely what this means. As soon as one steps out of the airport, there will be many who "glue" themselves to the luggage wanting to "help" the traveler even when the traveler needs no help.

In the midst of a "severe famine," the citizens did not need new workers. The citizen that the Prodigal approached was trying to get rid of him. But the Prodigal refused to leave. He "glued himself" to him because he was starving. We read at the end of verse 14 that he was "impoverished." The citizen recognized him to be Jewish and devised a plan to get rid of him- offer him a job to take care of the pigs! He thought that the moment the Jewish young man heard the word "pig," he would run away.[197] But, to his utter shock, the Prodigal accepted the job because he was desperate to eat. Yet, he could not satisfy his hunger. *"No one was giving anything to him"* is a very sad statement and once again illustrates the folly of serving sin.

Sin, while it looks glamorous and attractive, is a hard taskmaster. Once a person is enslaved by sin, reality sets in and all the glamor is gone. Just look around us. How many thousands commit suicide to escape the master to whom they gladly enslaved themselves? Jeffrey Epstein is just one example. *"... the wages of sin is death, but the free gift of God is eternal life in Christ Jesus our Lord."* Romans 6:23. But the sad fact remains that very few listen.

---

[197] *"Cursed is he who feeds swine"* was the prevalent attitude among the Jews. William Barclay, *The Gospel of Luke,* p. 204.

We know that the famine was sent by Father[198] to awaken the Prodigal from his slumber. Famine is the result of Father's love.

Scene #4: Severe Hunger Awakens Memory!

> [17] *"But when he came to his senses, he said, 'How many of my father's hired men have more than enough bread, but I am dying here with hunger!* [18] *'I will get up and go to my father, and will say to him, "Father, I have sinned against heaven, and in your sight;* [19] *I am no longer worthy to be called your son; make me as one of your hired men."* Luke 15:17-19.

This is a critical moment in the story. Some think that the Prodigal is repenting here when we read, "he came to his senses." But there is one serious objection to that view. The critically important New Testament word for repentance (metanoia) is not found here. While sitting in the pig pen, starving to death, suddenly he remembers:

> *"How many of my father's hired men have more than enough bread, but I am dying here with hunger!"*

What awakened his memory? Severe hunger caused by the severe famine! And how does he remember his father?

To fully understand the "memory" of the Prodigal, we need to know an important detail about a wealthy first-century home in Israel. A typical wealthy home had three

---

[198] Notice that I used Father with a capital F. We must not press a one-to-one correspondence with the father in the story and our heavenly Father.

kinds of servants. All three kinds appear in our story, indicating that the father was a wealthy man.

The first and most important kind of servants were known by the Greek word *doulos,* which means *slave.* Doulos was owned by the master and was part of his family. It is the Apostle Paul's favorite word to describe himself as the *doulos* of Jesus Christ. Doulos appears in verse 22 of the story.

The second group of servants was known by the Greek word *pais (singular; plural is paidos),* found in verse 26 and translated most of the time by the word "servant." He was a permanent employee of the master.

The third and considered least important was known by the Greek word *misthios* translated as "hired servant." These are temporary workers hired only when needed. These are men who stand idle in marketplaces, hoping to be hired by someone. Jesus told a parable about such people in Matthew 20:1 to 16. *Misthios* were not treated with kindness by most. They were the kind that would work for a day and get drunk for three days!

Yet, when the Prodigal in the pigpen, starving to death, remembers his father, he remembers him as a man who treats even the *misthios* with kindness. The verbal picture we see in verse 17 is the *misthios* swimming in bread. They have so much bread to eat that there is leftover! The Prodigal does not even get to eat what pigs eat! What a contrast between the father's house and where rebellion has led him!

In the father's house, there is plenty even for the "hired servants." But in the far country, the son is starving to death!

Thus, motivated by the desire to eat bread, the Prodigal decides to get out of the pigpen and return to the father. *It is very important to understand that what motivated the Prodigal is not the love for the father; it is love for bread!*

What or who planted the memory and motivation in his heart to get out of the pigpen?

This question was the focus of a major debate between St. Augustine (354-430 AD) and Pelagius (354-418 AD) in the fourth and fifth centuries. Pelagius pointed to the words, *"I will get up and go to my father..."* (Luke 15:18a) and argued that man is capable of doing good on his own.[199] He denied the Church's teaching on original sin that because of Adam's disobedience, humanity is incapable of obeying God unless God gives him *prevenient* grace. Augustine ingeniously pointed out that what gave the Prodigal the motivation and ability to get up was *the memory of his father*, a father who graciously dealt with even the *misthios*! If he remembered the father as a cruel man who mistreated people, he would not have returned to him. He remembered his father as a loving, caring person who cared for even the so-called "lowest" people. And who planted that memory in his heart and mind? *The father did!* This is the prevenient grace that enables us to respond to God's love.

---

[199] Islam also teaches the same and points to this text to "prove" that a man's salvation depends on his actions. The cross is not needed for humanity's salvation. As St. Augustine argued and will be seen soon, this is a terrible misreading of the story. It is the Father, "the Hound of Heaven," who was pursuing the Prodigal and who humiliates himself to rescue the Prodigal from the rightful punishment that ought to have fallen on him.

What the Prodigal says next is sure evidence that he has not grasped the father's heart or genuinely repented. He is getting out with a "plan" to *earn* bread from his father. Listen carefully to his pre-planned, three-point apology: *"I will get up and go to my father and will say to him,*

> a) *"Father, I have sinned against heaven, and in your sight;*
> b) *"I am no longer worthy to be called your son;"*
> c) *"make me as one of your hired men (misthios)."* Luke 15:18-19.[200]

Through the words of the Prodigal, Jesus is summarizing the central teaching of all the religions of the world. All human religions, including the religion of the Pharisees and scribes, teach the same despite all the apparent differences among them. They all agree on these three points.

> 1. Man is a sinner: *"Father, I have sinned against heaven, and in your sight. . ."*

> 2. Therefore, man has no right to enter the presence of God as His child: *"I am no longer worthy to be called your son. . ."*

> 3. Here is the solution to the problem: "Make *me as one of your hired men (misthios)."* Man must work to earn his salvation, his bread, if we may use the picture of the story.

This is precisely what the Pharisees and scribes taught. This is the teaching of all religions in the world

---

[200] Bailey, *Finding the Lost,* p. 149. "His expressed motive is a desire to eat. The prodigal returns home planning to save himself by his labor as a craftsman."

except the Gospel. Man must *earn* his Salvation, his Moksha, his Mukti.

In other words, work-righteousness is at the core of all religions except the Gospel.

If a Pharisee told the rest of the story, it would have gone something like the following:

"The Prodigal got up and went to the father. The father saw him from far away. Father got up, went inside, and locked the door of his room. The son came and knocked at the door. Father asked from inside: *"Who is knocking?"*

"This is your younger son. I have decided to come home. Will you please open the door for me?"

Father: "Are you clean? Are you dressed properly?"

Son: *"No, father. I am filthy. I am coming from the pigpen. I smell terrible, and I do not have any clean clothes."*

Father: *"Go clean yourself up. Get some good clothes. Then come back. I might consider opening the door for you!"*

That's precisely what the Pharisees were saying to the tax collectors and "sinners." They were not clean enough for God. They did not smell right to enter the presence of God. Tanners were branded as "sinners" for the obvious reason that their trade made them smell bad.[201]

---

[201] Acts chapter 10 describes the story of the conversion of an Italian centurion (an officer in the Roman military who commanded one hundred soldiers). Acts 9:43 tells us that Peter "stayed in Joppa for many days with one Simon, a tanner." We can assume that Peter is staying with Simon because Simon is a follower of Christ. Have you

In India, even today, chamars, a caste that has several million people, are considered the lowest of the lowest because they deal with the hide of animals!

That's what all the religions of the world are saying even today. Earn good *karma*. Go on pilgrimages! Wash yourself in this river or that at auspicious moments. Light candles. Give money! Do penance! The list goes on! All these are efforts to "earn bread" from God. Note that the Prodigal is saying make me a *"misthios,"* (a hired worker who was at the lowest strata of the society), not even a *"pais"* (a servant who had a permanent job) or "doulos" (a

---

wondered why Dr. Luke tells us the profession of the host of Peter, that he was a tanner? His name was Simon; therefore, we know he was a Jew. Jewish tanners were not allowed to enter the synagogue or the Temple because of their unclean profession. But now, as Simon the tanner is in Christ, Simon Peter, the Apostle of Christ, stays with him in his home, telling the whole world they are brothers in Christ.

It is while Peter is staying with Simon, the Tanner, that he receives the revelation of the "sheet from heaven" with all kinds of unclean creatures and hears the command: *"Rise, Peter; kill and eat."* (Acts 10:13). Peter, who strictly kept the Jewish rules of Kosher food, refused, saying: *"By no means, Lord, for I have never eaten anything that is common or unclean."* (Acts 10:14). In response to his objection, the Lord told him: *"What God has made clean, do not call common."* (Acts 10:15). Soon, there were Italians, who were considered "dirty" by Peter because of their food habits, knocking at the door of Simon's house. The Holy Spirit directed Peter to go with them, and Peter obeyed. This led to the doors of the Church being opened to Gentiles and the Holy Spirit falling on Italians just as the Holy Spirit baptized the Jewish believers on the day of Pentecost. (Acts 10:44-48). It is important to note that it is after Peter overcame his prejudice against fellow Jewish tanners, who were rejected by Pharisees and scribes as "unclean," that he received the further revelation that God also loves the Gentile Italians who do not eat Kosher food!

slave: by virtue of being owned by the master, a member of the family)!

How differently Jesus tells the story! Let's listen!

Scene #5 Prodigal Comes Home from the Pigpen:

> *20 "So he got up and came to his father. But while he was still a long way off, his father saw him and felt compassion for him, and ran and embraced him and kissed him. 21 "And the son said to him, 'Father, I have sinned against heaven and in your sight; I am no longer worthy to be called your son.' 22 "But the father said to his slaves, 'Quickly bring out the best robe and put it on him, and put a ring on his hand and sandals on his feet; 23 and bring the fattened calf, kill it, and let us eat and celebrate; 24 for this son of mine was dead and has come to life again; he was lost and has been found.' And they began to celebrate."* Luke 15:20-24.

What his audience heard from the mouth of Jesus must have shocked them and surprised them. Both the Pharisees and "the people of the land" expected an angry father just as the Prodigal expected because that was the common notion about God as it is in our own day: "the angry, frowning man upstairs."

The father was watching and waiting for the return of his beloved son. *"While he was still a long way off, his father saw him…" (verse 20).* Then comes a word that is so rich that it would take a long time to fully expound it.

It is translated into English with the words: "felt compassion" (ESV and NASB), "filled with compassion" (NIV, NRSV), or "had compassion" (KV). The original text has only one word: ἐσπλαγχνίσθη esplagchnisthē coming from the word σπλαγχνίζομαι splagchnizomai. It is

239

worth our while to spend a little time to understand this very important New Testament word.

This word is found only twelve times in the New Testament, and that too only in the first three Gospels (Synoptic Gospels).[202] Moreover, it is found only either about Jesus (nine times) or in his mouth (three times in three of his parables: parable of the merciful king and unmerciful servant in Matthew 18, parable of the Good Samaritan in Luke 10, and the parable we are studying). That fact alone ought to alert us that it is a unique word.

It is a very powerful word. Wherever it is used in the New Testament, either Jesus or the character in the story he tells does something totally unexpected and changes the situation. For example, the word is used in Mark 1:41, where a leper came to Christ and begged him on his knees: *"If you are willing, you can make me clean."* Then we hear these shocking words for the ears of a first-century, religious Jewish audience: *"Filled with compassion (σπλαγχνίζομαι splagchnizomai), Jesus reached out his hand and touched the man."* A leper was considered unclean, and touching him was against the Old Testament teaching. They were not permitted within the camp of Israel (Numbers 5:2; even Miriam, Moses' own sister, was put out of the camp for seven days when she became leprous. Numbers 12: 14. See also Leviticus 13:45-46).

Father is full of this compassion towards all his children.

---

[202] Matthew 9:36; 14:14; 15:32; 18:27; 20:34; Mark 1:41; 6:34; 8:2; 9:22; Luke 7:13; 10:33; and 15:20.

Scene #6 Father Running: Picture of the Cross.

"...his father saw him and felt compassion for him, and ran and embraced him and kissed him." Luke 15:20b.

Once again, most of us read on as if nothing dramatic or unusual is happening here because of our ignorance of the culture. In the West, public running by all ages of people is so very common. So, we do not think much of it when we read that the father ran to receive his returning son. Not so with the audience of Jesus. They could not believe their ears because they knew that no self-respecting Oriental nobleman would run in public.[203]

When my own elderly parents visited and stayed with us in California in the 1980s, we had a similar experience. My parents lived all their lives in a small village in South India and were used to people coming and visiting them and sitting around and talking with them. One of the major culture shocks they experienced in the US was not seeing people walking down the streets as is common back home. My father would often open our front door and stand on the porch looking for people. He would ask me: "Where are the people?" as he could only see cars going back and forth.

One day, as he was standing on the porch, he saw one of our older neighbors running. He came inside with excitement and called my mother to come out, almost shouting: *"Come! Come! See, here is an old man running!"* He couldn't believe his eyes that an older person would run! He wanted my mother to see it; otherwise, she

---

[203] Bailey, *Poet & Peasant,* P. 181

wouldn't believe him! In my parents' culture, an elderly man was not supposed to run, just like in the days of Jesus!

Bailey quotes Ben Sirach: *"A man's manner of walking tells you what he is."* A commentator by the name L. P. Weatherhead is quoted by Bailey as saying: *"It is so very undignified in Eastern eyes for an elderly man to run. Aristotle says, 'Great men never run in public.'"*[204]

Thus, what the father did was shocking to the audience of Jesus.

Why did he run? Was it just because of his excitement to see his long-lost son again? Yes, of course. But there was more to it.

The wealthy father's house was in the middle of the village, as is typical in a Middle Eastern village. The houses of workers and others were around the father's house.

When the Prodigal left the village, he turned his back on the entire community, not just the father and the brother. Now he is coming back after losing everything. Even if the *qesasah* ('Cutting Off") ceremony was not done when he left, many would want to do it now as he has returned as a loser![205]

The moment the returning Prodigal steps into the village, news will spread to all, like wildfire, and a mob will gather. The gathering of a mob and slander by a whole town are two things that terrified even a sage like Ben

---

[204] Bailey, *Poet & Peasant,* P. 181.

[205] See above Scene #2.

Sirach. [206] Once a mob gathers, the returning Prodigal will be cruelly insulted. They will taunt him and ask him all kinds of denigrating questions. The father knew all these well. He wanted to protect his beloved child from such a treatment. *That's why he ran.* By running, he drew attention to himself and took the humiliation upon himself; the loving father was protecting his beloved child. *He was taking upon himself the shame that rightfully ought to have fallen on the Prodigal!*

Thus, the Father running toward the Prodigal is the picture of the Cross of Christ.

The picture of the Father running in order to protect his beloved child from the cruel words and deeds of insults by the gathering mob is part of what Isaiah saw centuries before the Crucifixion.

> *"Surely he has borne our griefs*
> *and carried our sorrows;*
> *yet we esteemed him stricken,*
> *smitten by God, and afflicted.*
> *But he was pierced for our transgressions;*
> *he was crushed for our iniquities;*
> *upon him was the chastisement that brought us*
> *peace,*
> *and with his wounds we are healed.*
> *All we like sheep have gone astray;*
> *we have turned—every one—to his own way;*
> *and the LORD has laid on him*
> *the iniquity of us all." Isaiah 53:4-6.*

---

[206] Bailey, *Poet & Peasant,* p. 181.

Scene #7 Transformation of the Prodigal

> *"And the son said to him, 'Father, I have sinned against heaven and in your sight; I am no longer worthy to be called your son.' 22 "But the father said to his slaves, 'Quickly bring out the best robe and put it on him, and put a ring on his hand and sandals on his feet; 23 and bring the fattened calf, kill it, and let us eat and celebrate; 24 for this son of mine was dead and has come to life again; he was lost and has been found.' And they began to celebrate.* Luke 15:21-24.

The Prodigal came home with fear and trembling, not knowing what kind of reception awaited him. He expected to face an angry father who might reject him and punish him. His best hope was to become a *misthios* (a hired servant) of the father and try to give back by working for him and in the process eat and not starve to death. He knew fully well that he deserved to be punished for what he did and might have fully expected the *qesasah* ('Cutting Off') ceremony and humiliation. But when he saw his father running towards him, all his fears vanished. For the first time in his life, the Prodigal understood how much his father loved him. He realized that his father loved him enough to take upon himself the shame and humiliation that he earned and deserved. *The sight of the Father running to receive him, which is the picture of the Cross of Christ, is what caused the repentance of the Prodigal.*

Remember, he came with a three-point "confession" with a built-in solution for his rebellion. Look what happened to his pre-planned speech. The third point is missing in his confession to his father. *"And the son said to him, 'Father, I have sinned against heaven and in your sight; I am no longer worthy to be called your son."* (Luke 15:21).

Baily quotes Ibn al-Salibi, "a giant of Biblical interpretation in the Syriac tradition":

> *"Why did he (the prodigal) not say to his father, "Fashion out of me one of your paid craftsmen," when he had planned to say it? The answer is that his father's love outstripped him and forgiveness was overflowing toward him."*[207]

The missing third point is *the evidence of his genuine repentance.*[208]

We can say that the Prodigal was born again the moment he saw his father running to receive him. He is no longer proposing to be treated as a "misthios" because he

---

[207] Bailey, Finding the Lost, p. 153.

[208] Traditional interpretation, especially Western, is that the father interrupted the Prodigal and did not allow him to complete his confession. That is missing one of the most critical points that the parable is making. Seeing his father humiliating himself by running in public to protect him from the insults and wounding words that he deserved, the prodigal, for the first time in his life, began to grasp the enormity of the father's love for him. That sight transformed him from a self-seeking, callous person who cared only for "bread." A genuine love for the father gripped him. In the words of Bailey: ". . . faced with this incredible event, he is flooded with the awareness that his real sin is not the lost money but rather the wounded heart. *The reality and enormity of his sin and the resulting intensity of his father's suffering overwhelm him.* In a flash of awareness, he now knows that there is nothing he can do to make up for what he has done. **His proposed offer to work as a servant now seems blasphemous.** He is not interrupted. He changes his mind and accepts being found." *The Cross & the Prodigal,* p. 70. Emphasis added. Only when we see the Cross of Calvary will we truly understand the enormity of our sins and genuinely repent. Here, Jesus masterfully paints the picture of his imminent cross.

understood that the father loved him way too much for that and that he was being received back ONLY because of the father's unconditional love for him.

Father falls on his neck and kisses him again and again. He barely pays attention to the Prodigal's confession. Notice the word "but" (δέ-de- in the original) at the beginning of verse 22: *"**But** the father said to his slaves. . ."* Instead of paying attention to the son's confession, the father turns to the "slaves" *(douloi)*. By now there is a crowd all around the Prodigal and the father, including all of the father's slaves *(douloi)* and other household members. Father orders his slaves:

> *"Quickly bring out the best robe and put it on him, and put a ring on his hand and sandals on his feet; 23 and bring the fattened calf, kill it, and let us eat and celebrate; 24 for this son of mine was dead and has come to life again; he was lost and has been found.' And they began to celebrate."* Luke 15:22-24.

Notice the four specific orders of the father:

- a) "Bring out the best robe and put it on him.
- b) Put a ring on his hand.
- c) (Put) sandals on his feet.
- d) Bring the fattened calf, kill it..."

Each of the items has symbolic meaning.

a) The best robe.

"The best robe" is the father's robe.[209] By putting his own robe on the Prodigal, the father was declaring to the

---

[209] "The best robe is most certainly the Father's. The Oriental listener/reader would immediately assume this. The "first" (i.e., best)

246

whole world that he is accepting his son back as his son. There is a clear reference to the famous Old Testament passages of Isaiah 61:10 and Zechariah 3:3-5 here.[210]

Notice also that the father did not ask the Prodigal to go and clean himself up before putting on him his own robe. This once again stands in contrast to the teaching of all other religions that man has to clean himself up before God would accept him. One can come to the father just as he is and he will accept him unconditionally.

b) Ring.

The ring represents the authority to sign checks, to use our contemporary language. It is the signet ring, the kind of

---

robe would be the robe the father wore on feast days and other grand occasions." Bailey, Poet & Peasant, p. 185.

[210] *Is. 61:10   I will greatly rejoice in the LORD, my soul shall be joyful in my God; for he hath clothed me with the garments of salvation, he hath covered me with the robe of righteousness, as a bridegroom decketh himself with ornaments, and as a bride adorneth herself with her jewels. (KJV)*

Zech. 3:3-5 *Now Joshua was standing before the angel, clothed with filthy garments. ⁴ And the angel said to those who were standing before him, "Remove the filthy garments from him." And to him he said, "Behold, I have taken your iniquity away from you, and I will clothe you with pure vestments." ⁵ And I said, "Let them put a clean turban on his head." So they put a clean turban on his head and clothed him with garments. And the angel of the LORD was standing by. (ESV).*

ring that Pharoah put on Joseph's fingers in Genesis 41:42[211] See also Esther 3:10; 8:2 and 8.

What does the father do when the Prodigal who took his share of the property and wasted all of it in "wild living" comes back? He gives him the family bank account! That's what the ring represents. What extravagant love and grace!

c) Sandals.

Sandals are the clear mark of sonship. No servant, even the highest in rank (doulos), was permitted to wear sandals. Therefore, the father's order to put sandals on the feet of the returning Prodigal is another public declaration for all to see that he is being fully and completely reinstated as son and heir and not as a servant.

One of the famous American Negro spirituals written during the slavery days helps us to understand the significance of shoes/sandals. None of the slaves were permitted to wear shoes/sandals. So they sang

"I got shoes, you got shoes,
All God's children got shoes.
When I get to Heav'n gonna put in my shoes,
Gonna walk all over God's Heav'n, Heav'n, Heav'n..."[212]

---

[211] Gen. 41:41-43. "So Pharaoh said to Joseph, "I hereby put you in charge of the whole land of Egypt." [42] Then Pharaoh took his signet ring from his finger and put it on Joseph's finger. He dressed him in robes of fine linen and put a gold chain around his neck. [43] He had him ride in a chariot as his second-in-command, and people shouted before him, "Make way!" Thus he put him in charge of the whole land of Egypt."

[212] From http://etl.du.edu/spirituals/freedom/protest.cfm "Spirituals As Expressions of Protest. Accessed on January 12, 2024. The first stanza is also noteworthy as it talks about a robe.

d) Fattened calf.

The killing of a calf (and not a goat or a sheep) indicates that the celebration is going to be huge.[213] The whole community is invited as the father wants everyone to know that his lost son is back.

Some have tried to see the death of Christ in the killing of the calf. But that is totally wrong, as the killing of the calf happens after the Prodigal is restored to the father. It is part of the celebrations and signifies the great joy of finding the lost son. It is the father who paid the price to redeem and reconcile the lost son.

Part Two: The Older Son

> [25] *"Now his older son was in the field, and when he came and approached the house, he heard music and dancing.* [26] *"And he summoned one of the servants and began inquiring what these things could be.* [27] *"And he said to him, 'Your brother has come, and your father has killed the fattened calf because he has received him back safe and sound.'* [28] *"But he became angry and was not willing to go in; and his father came out and began pleading with him.* [29] *"But he answered and said to his father, 'Look! For so many years I have been serving you and I have never neglected a command of yours; and yet you have never given me a young goat, so that I might celebrate with my friends;* [30]

"I got a robe, you got a robe,
All God's children got a robe.
When I get to Heav'n gonna put in my robe,
Gonna shout all over God's Heav'n, Heav'n, Heav'n..."

[213] Bailey, *Poet & Peasant,* p. `186.

but when this son of yours came, who has devoured your wealth with prostitutes, you killed the fattened calf for him.' 31 "And he said to him, 'Son, you have always been with me, and all that is mine is yours. 32 'But we had to celebrate and rejoice, for this brother of yours was dead and has begun to live, and was lost and has been found." Luke 15:25-32.

Scene #1: The Older Son Comes Home from the Field:

25 "Now his older son was in the field, and when he came and approached the house, he heard music and dancing. 26 "And he summoned one of the servants and began inquiring what these things could be. 27 "And he said to him, 'Your brother has come, and your father has killed the fattened calf because he has received him back safe and sound.' Luke 15:25-27.

As the celebrations are going on in the house, the older son returns home from the field after a day's hard work. As he approached the house, he heard "music and dancing." Words in the Greek text are the words from which we get the English words symphony and choreography![214] The music and dancing in the father's house are classy!

Now, if the older son's relationship with the father was good, he would have walked straight into his house to find out the reason for the music and dancing. None of us will call our neighbors to ask what is happening in our own homes if we hear music and dancing when we return from the office, will we? NO! We will march straight into our homes and find out. The very fact that the older son called

---

[214] συμφωνία (sumphōnia) and χορός (choros).

one of the servants *(pais)* and asked him what was going on in his own house raises all kinds of red flags to the hearer. As noted earlier, these red flags were visible right at the beginning of the story. Now they become all the more apparent and troubling.

The servant *(pais)*[215] reported to him the whole story: *"Your brother has come, and your father has killed the fattened calf because he has received him back safe and sound."* (Verse 27).

The older brother ought to have jumped up and down with joy and should have run inside and kissed his brother, and joined in the party. That would have been the natural reaction of a loving brother if his long-lost brother is found and is back safe and sound. But that is not what Jesus said, as you know.

Scene #2 The Angry Son and the Father who Humbles Himself (Picture of the Angry Pharisees and Scribes and the Loving Father/Jesus).

To the utter shock of his audience, Jesus said:

"But he became angry and was not willing to go in; and his father came out and began pleading with him" (verse 28).

The broken relationship with the father is becoming visible to all through the angry outburst of the older son. What the older son is doing -becoming angry in the presence of all to see and refusing to go in and join the joyous celebration that the father has organized- *is insulting*

---

[215] There is a lengthy discussion about the exact identity of the servant (pais) in Bailey, *The Cross & the Prodigal,* p. 79-80 and in *Poet & Peasant,* p. 193-194.

the father. In the context of the Middle East, this is an unpardonable act- insulting one's own father in public. The younger son's rejection of the father's love started in private. The older son's rejection and insult of the father is in front of all the servants and other public.

What the older son does is equally or more atrocious and deplorable than what the younger one did!

Listen to the words of Ibn al-Tayyib, an eminent Christian scholar from the Middle East thoroughly familiar with the original languages of the Scripture and culture of the land:

> *"(In his refusal to enter,) the older son demonstrated maliciousness of character and meanness. He has no love for his brother and no appropriate respect for his father. His position in this regard is equivalent to the grumbling of the scribes and Pharisees against the Christ for acceptance of sinners."*[216]

A typical Eastern father would have said something like the following when the news of the angry older son's refusal to enter the house was reported to him: *"Okay. If he doesn't want to come in, let him stand out there!"*

Or worse, as Bailey reports, *"would order his slaves to overpower the disobedient son in the courtyard and drag him by force into a side room and lock him up. After the guests had left, the older son would be brought out, held down by the slaves, and beaten."*[217]

---

[216] Bailey, *Finding the Lost,* p. 171.

[217] Bailey, *Finding the Lost,* p. 172.

This father is radically different. Once again, he does what is least expected from a father of his stature. The father who ran to receive the openly rebellions younger son humiliates himself once again to go out and plead with the older son who has just insulted him in the presence of his guests and servants! He humbles himself and goes out searching for his older son with the same kind of love and compassion that he showed to the younger son. There is no partiality with the father![218]

All of Jesus' audience knew instinctively that no father among them would EVER tolerate such behavior from any of their children. But this father's forgiveness and love are unfathomable. The angry and self-righteous attitude of the older son immediately brings to our mind the angry response of Jonah to God's forgiving grace.[219] The prophet ought to have rejoiced that because of his preaching one hundred and twenty thousand people turned to God and were spared from the wrath of God. But because of his ethnocentric attitude and blatant racism, Jonah could not comprehend the amazing grace of God. So, instead of praising God and thanking him for his mercy and grace, Jonah became angry. The older son's attitude is very similar to that of Jonah.

---

[218] Romans 2:11; Acts 10:34; Galatians 2:6; Ephesians 6:9. Acts 10:34-35 is particularly relevant here: *"Then Peter began to speak: "I now realize how true it is that God does not show favoritism but accepts from every nation the one who fears him and does what is right."*

[219] Jonah 4:1-11.

Scene #3 The Self-righteous Son and the Self-emptying Father:[220]

29 "But he answered and said to his father, 'Look! For so many years I have been serving you and I have never neglected a command of yours; and yet you have never given me a young goat, so that I might celebrate with my friends; 30 but when this son of yours came, who has devoured your wealth with prostitutes, you killed the fattened calf for him.' 31 "And he said to him, 'Son, you have always been with me, and all that is mine is yours. 32 'But we had to celebrate and rejoice, for this brother of yours was dead and has begun to live, and was lost and has been found." Luke 15:29-32.

In this part of the story, there is a critical difference between the younger son and the older son. When the younger son saw the self-sacrificing love of the father, he responded by repenting. He threw away his prepared speech and opened his heart in genuine confession. In other words, he understood and accepted the love of the father. We can also say that "he allowed the father to find him" or "he received the father's love."

But the response of the older son is completely different. When the father comes out to "plead"[221] with

---

[220] We hear the echoes of Philippians 2:5ff in the actions and words of the father.

[221] Once again, note the careful use of words by Jesus (Dr. Luke). The father ought to have commanded him as a typical Eastern father would. But this father is different. He "pleads" with his son. Luke uses the word parekalei (παρεκάλει) from parakaleō (παρακαλέω) translated as "pleaded" (NIV, NASB, NRSV), "entreated" (ESV). It is the same word that Jairus uses in Luke 8:40 to plead with Jesus to help his

254

him, thus humiliating himself, *the older son does not change; he continues his disrespectful behavior!* The way he addresses him ("Look!" ESV, NIV, NASB; "Listen" NRSV; "Lo" KJV; ἰδοὺ idou in the original) without any title is highly insulting and disrespectful.[222] One NEVER addresses one's father with such a term in the East.

> *'Look! For so many years I have been serving you..* (verses 29a).

First, notice how he describes himself: *"I have been serving you..."* The word used is douleuō (δουλεύω), which means *"to serve as a slave"!* It is also very important to note that the tense of the verb is present active indicative, meaning that he is still continuing in the mentality of a slave though he is a son. He saw himself as a slave (*doulos*). It is a sad fact that there are many in the Church who live as "slaves" trying to please the father by their work instead of allowing the father to embrace them and make them children.

Then comes another shocking statement:

"I have never neglected a command of yours..." *(verse 29b).*   While disrespecting and humiliating his father, he claims that he has NEVER neglected any of his commands! This is simultaneously a very humorous and tragic picture. Jesus is painting the picture of Pharisees and scribes. They claimed to be "perfectly righteous."[223] At the same time, they looked down upon their own flesh and

---

daughter. That is the only other use of the word parakaleō (παρακαλέω) in the Gospel of Luke.

[222] Bailey, *Poet & Peasant,* p. 196.

[223] See footnote 175.

blood: the shepherds, the tax collectors, the tanners, etc., and hated them as sinners. By hating them, they were violating the most important of all commandments: "... you shall love your neighbor as yourself: I am the LORD." Leviticus 19:18.

> *"...and yet you have never given me a young goat, so that I might celebrate with my friends."*

His disrespectful attitude becomes even clearer when he affirms that he has never received anything from his father. His lack of gratitude toward the father, who has evidently cared for him all these years, becomes apparent.

> *"...but when this son of yours came, who has devoured your wealth with prostitutes, you killed the fattened calf for him."* (verse 30).

The older son goes beyond insulting his father and expressing his lack of gratitude to him; he also slanders his brother. His expression *"this son of yours"* to describe his brother shows the total break in his relationship with his only sibling. Then he continues to accuse his brother of things that are nowhere intimated in the story: that his brother *"devoured"* the father's property with *prostitutes*! This is slander to the highest possible degree. How did he know this? Thus, the older brother's words reveal his fractured relationship with his father *and* brother.

The father's response to the insults and accusations of his older son is filled with love and grace, just as his actions toward the younger son were. While the older son calls his brother "this son of yours," the father gently reminds him of his responsibility toward his brother by describing him as "this brother of yours!"

While the older son refused to use a respectful title to address his father, the father addresses him with a very tender title: *teknon* (τέκνον), child. It is the same word that Mary, the mother of Jesus, uses to address him when she and Joseph found him in the Temple after searching for him among their relatives and friends for three days. (Luke 2:48). Here, we see the amazing love of the father who searches for the lost son.

The story closes without a conclusion. Did the older son enter the banquet? Tune in next week to find out!!! Jesus, the master storyteller, leaves us in suspense.

The conclusion is to be written by each one of us. How do we respond to the father's love? We can either receive it or reject it.

When we look at all three stories together, *we come to a more perfect understanding of repentance.* In the first two stories, it is being found. The lost sheep and the lost coin are found. When we come to the final story, we understand it is more than being found. *It is also accepting being found.*

The younger son accepted the father's embrace and genuinely repented. Did the older son allow the father to "find" him and embrace him?

Another important lesson is that we cannot love the father without loving the brother. This truth becomes more explicit in the later New Testament revelation. We read in 1 John 4:20 and 21:

> *"If anyone says, "I love God," and hates his brother, he is a liar; for he who does not love his brother whom he has seen cannot love God whom he has not seen. [21] And this commandment we have from him: whoever loves God must also love his brother."*

May the Lord give us grace to understand what true repentance is! May we be found by Him! And may we allow Him to find us! May He protect us from hypocrisy, looking down on others and treating them as less than human! May we love God with all of our heart, mind, soul, and strength and love our neighbors as ourselves!

Bibliography

Kenneth Bailey, *Finding the Lost: Cultural Keys to Luke 15.* St. Louis, MO. Concordia Publishing, 1992.

Kenneth Bailey, *Jacob and the Prodigal.* Downers Grove, IL. Intervarsity Press, 2003.

Kenneth Bailey, *Jesus Through Middle Eastern Eyes-Cultural Studies in the Gospels.* Downers Grove, IL. IVP Academic, 2008.

Kenneth Bailey, *Poet and Peasant & Through Peasant Eyes: A Literary-Cultural Approach to the Parables in Luke.* Eerdmans Publishing Co., Grand Rapids, MI. 1983.

Kenneth Bailey, *The Cross and the Prodigal: Luke 15 Through the Eyes of Middle Eastern Peasants.* Downers Grove, IL. Intervarsity Press, 2005.

Kenneth Bailey, *The Good Shepherd: A Thousand Year Journey from Psalm 23 to the New Testament.* Downers Grove, IL. IVP Academic. 2014.

William Barclay, *The Gospel of Luke, Revised Edition.* The Westminster Press, Philadelphia, PA. 1975.

F. Dale Bruner, *A Tale of Two Sons: The Wastrel and the "Presbyterian": A Parable Revised, Christianity Today,* October 4, 1985.

Norval Geldenhuys, *Commentary on the Gospel of Luke,* The New International Commentary on the New Testament. Eerdmans Publishing Co., Grand Rapids, MI. 1951.

Joachim Jeremias, *Jerusalem in the Time of Jesus.* Philadelphia, PA. Fortress Press, 1969.

Christopher J.H. Wright, *The Mission of God: Unlocking the Bible's Grand Narrative,* Downers Grove, IL: Intervarsity Press, 2006.

Please pray for India and for the ministries of Good News for India.

To know more about us please contact:

**Good News for India
PO Box 7576
La Verne, CA 91750**

www.goodnewsforindia.org

**Email us at:
george@goodnewsforindia.com or**

gnficea@gmail.com

**Thank you, and
may the Lord bless you!**

About the Author

George Kuruvilla Chavanikamannil, endearingly called by many as "Uncle" George, with his wife, Leela, founded the ministries of Good News for India (GNFI) in 1986 after leaving his career with World Vision USA.

God used George and Leela with George's nephew, The Rev. George C. Kuruvilla, to found Bharat Susamachar Samiti (BSS), the parent body of New Theological College (NTC), Khrist Jyoti group of schools (KJA), and Jeevan Jyoti Bal Vikas (JJBV) projects that care for hundreds of needy children.

God also used them to pioneer Christian Evangelistic Assemblies (CEA). CEA has several hundred congregations in India and Nepal.

George is an ordained minister with Grace International Churches and Ministries, which has nearly five thousand churches worldwide.

He holds degrees from the University of Kerala, India (BA in Philosophy; MA in English Language and Literature), Fuller Theological Seminary, Pasadena, California (Master of Divinity), Gordon-Conwell Theological Seminary, South Hamilton, Massachusetts (Doctor of Ministry), and Serampore College (University), Serampore, India (Doctor of Divinity, Honorary Causa).

Made in the USA
Columbia, SC
14 February 2024

31398681R10143